How dare you BE so GORGEOUS!

Write your name here:

....

If your light gets lost,
where can you be found?

....

....

How dare you be
so gorgeous!

SHINE
A GUIDED JOURNAL
YOUR
FOR DEEPENING YOUR
LIGHT
EMOTIONAL INTELLIGENCE

LUCINDA LIGHT

HarperCollins*Publishers*

HarperCollins*Publishers*
1 London Bridge Street
London SE1 9GF

www.harpercollins.co.uk

HarperCollins*Publishers*
Macken House, 39/40 Mayor Street Upper
Dublin 1, D01 C9W8, Ireland

First published by HarperCollins*Publishers* 2025

10 9 8 7 6 5 4 3 2 1

A catalogue record of this book is available from the British Library

ISBN 978-0-00-874161-7

Printed and bound by GPS Group in Bosnia and Herzegovina

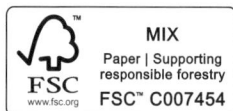

MIX
Paper | Supporting responsible forestry
FSC™ C007454
FSC
www.fsc.org

This book is produced from FSC™ certified paper and other controlled sources to ensure responsible forest management.

For more information visit: www.harpercollins.co.uk/green

To Spirit, Source, and the Universal Flow that has guided me in this lifetime. My heart is full of gratitude. This earthly adventure is a privilege, and I'm humbled to be a conduit of love and light.

• • •

With profound respect and gratitude, I'd like to honour the Indigenous and First Nations peoples of the world – past, present, and emerging. Your ancient wisdom, forged through millennia of connection to country, land, and spirit, is a beacon of resilience, inspiration, and hope.

Your stories, traditions, and ways of being illuminate a path forward for all humanity – a path rooted in respect, reciprocity, and care for the Earth and its interconnectedness. May we listen with open hearts, walk with humility, and commit to learning from your wisdom.

CONTENTS

RELATIONSHIPS

SHINE ON

WORDS ARE SPELLS

WELCOME!

Welcome to the journey: you've committed, you've begun!
Ready for a deep dive? Oh, there's so much to be spun!
With every page, you'll sketch, write, and uncover what is true –
It's time to shine your light and just be the fabulous you!

Be bold with your style and let your pen run wild,
Deliberate, cursive – let your creativity be compiled.
In this digital world, where thumbs mostly do the tap,
Let's reclaim pen and paper – it's time to unwrap!

In this paper-based adventure, this is your sacred place, so don't hide,
Decorate each page with love and let your authenticity roam inside.
Words are spells, so let your pen be your magic wand,
Every effort counts – do your best; let your heart respond!

Welcome soul-seeker! I want to speak directly to you – gorgeous you! Let's shine together and create a world brimming with soulful connections and boundless love, all fuelled by our growing emotional intelligence.

If you've been feeling like the world's missing a little something lately – a spark of purpose, connection, or magic – I totally get it. This guided journal is an invitation for us to walk this journey together toward something more awesome and authentic. I will share moments from my life and the tools that have helped me build more emotional intelligence, self-awareness, and resilience.

I'm still massively on that journey, it's never-ending – I'm a work in progress, as they say. And that's totally okay. The beauty is in the unfolding, in being willing to keep growing. You picking up what I'm putting down? YeeeeHaaaaaaa ... welcome, welcome, welcome!

• • •

The first thing I want to say is that you are *just gorgeous as you are, right now!* We are all on our own soul journey: each of us has our own individual divine purpose – the thing we are here to learn and do in this lifetime. *My* purpose is to share love and light and rejoice in how magnificent *you* are. And just how much more beauty can be revealed from the inside ... if you choose to explore your inner self.

Day-to-day life is so fast-paced: there are ideas and people and changes and news and pressures and leisure options flying at us from all directions. Sometimes, we need to make some space to really get to know ourselves better, layer by layer, unlearn/learn and get back to our truest, most authentic version. So, this book is where we can do that together; it isn't me telling you how to live, it's me inviting you to voyage right alongside me. Because no one else can tell you what your path should look like. What we can do is inspire each other, reflect back some truths, and love and support each other along the way. It's about finding a way to live more enthusiastically, discovering what truly lights you up, and letting that shine ripple out into your world (no pressure, ha!).

You with me, divine creature? I truly believe in our ability to make positive changes in our lives, and journalling can be so instrumental in that. So, let's talk, let's explore, and let's get positively pumped about where this path takes us. We're in this together, and I can't wait for what's ahead. Come with me down the yellow brick road ... a better version of Oz awaits!

This isn't a regular book – it has a choose-your-own-adventure approach! There's no set timeline here, no rigid rules to follow. Whether you start at the very beginning, dive into the middle, or flip to a random page that calls your name, it's all up to you. Make this journey your own.

Better yet, make a commitment with a close love who wants to embark on *Shine Your Light* too and turn this into a shared exploration. Set special dates to work through this journal together, cheering each other on and holding each other accountable. Let it be a celebration of growth, connection, and the radiant light within you both. Encourage each other to shine brighter than ever before.

Get creative! Colour in my illustrations; colour outside the lines; soulfully scribble on the borders. Add your own flair with notes, sketches, or collages that reflect your vibe. And please tag me on iG: @lucindaslight – I want to see pictures! Bookmark the pages that resonate most deeply, so you can revisit them as touchstones along your journey. Over time, the marks you leave will become a living record of your evolution – proof of how far you've come and where your heart is leading you next.

• • •

Before you start, take a moment to think about the word 'reflect'. The act – and art – of reflection is woven through every page of this book because it is the building block of learning. When we reflect – whether for seconds, minutes, or hours – we press pause. We create space not just to consider and process information but to invite in new ideas and therefore to foster insights. Reflection is the DNA of a growth mindset.

Putting pen to paper is a beautiful reflection strategy. It can be immensely powerful, allowing you to explore, build self-knowledge, and envision the 'future you'. So, pour your authentic spirit into these pages. Take your time and let your words and imagery flow wild and free, filled with love and truth and possibility.

This book is designed for you to engage with stories and ideas about emotional intelligence, so you can rewrite your own. It is full of gentle encouragement to choose and try transformative experiences. My starting point is personal reflections from my own journey, and I follow these with a wealth of inspiration, suggestions, and practical tools to illuminate your path. If any of these speak to you, try the activities, then take the opportunity to reflect on how it went and to deepen your self-awareness. There is no wrong response or outcome: every emotion is data – an opportunity to learn.

Each entry invites you to explore new layers of emotional intelligence, offering insights that can enrich your life. Like you, I'm still learning, and I recognise that some of the suggestions may feel a bit aspirational. But you can always look into them further next time around: the path of learning is more of a spiral than a straight road. Trust that as you become aware of possibility, open yourself to trying new things, and take the time to reflect, you'll find both wonderful and challenging opportunities arise for you. You can then journal about these, practise more, and adapt to find the best way to express your gorgeous, unique self.

By the end of this journey, my hope is that you'll feel more aligned with your true self, more emotionally aware, and you will be shining brighter than ever before.

• • •

With so much I want to share with you, I know there might not be enough space here for all your thoughts, reflections, and creative expressions. Feel free to add extra pages, stick in inserts, or even grab a separate notebook for those moments when you think, 'Lucinda! I need more room for this!' This is your personal journey, and you deserve all the space in the world to capture and explore your insights, emotions, and ideas. Let your self-expression flow freely.

• • •

Before you dive in, take a moment to centre yourself. Hold the book in your hands, and let your intuition guide you. Flip through until something speaks to you – that's your inner wisdom at work. Trust your instincts, and let them lead the way.

So, be true. Be you. Be free. Savour every moment of discovery, reflection, and transformation as you beam out more of your own light. And never forget – you are utterly divine! How dare you be so gorgeous!

Let's begin.

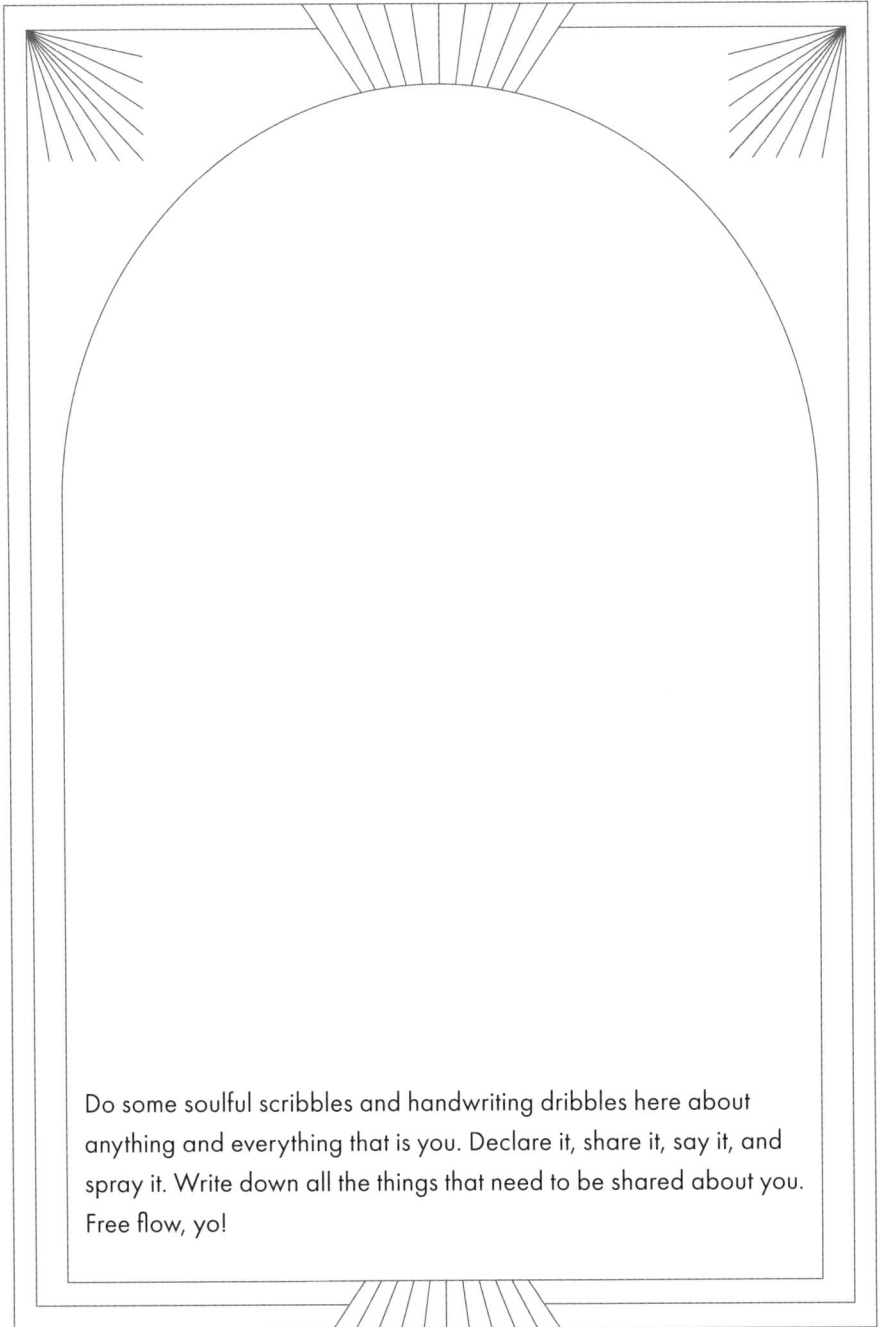

Do some soulful scribbles and handwriting dribbles here about anything and everything that is you. Declare it, share it, say it, and spray it. Write down all the things that need to be shared about you. Free flow, yo!

Though I may never read your words,
the marks you make on these pages send
waves of love and intention out into the Universe.
Like the ripples that flow outward when a pebble is
dropped in the still lake. Your words matter. You matter.
This journal is a reflection of you, so explore widely,
have a good look at what lies beneath, and don't hold back.
Be fully present in every sacred moment you spend with it, and
know in every fibre of your being that you are loved
and supported. Your journey is important, and your voice
deserves to be heard – both by yourself and the
world around you.

Divine Disclaimer

Gorgeous ...

This book is a call for you to step fully into your light and embrace the sacred, beautiful being that you already are. If things are more serious for you, though, please first get some professional help as your base. If you're carrying heavy stuff, like trauma or mental health struggles, it's essential to access the right support from professionals who are trained to help you navigate those waters. Your GP is a good place to start.

I'm a soul mama and holistic counsellor, but I'm not a qualified trauma counsellor or psychological practitioner. The insights I offer in this book are based on my own experiences; so, it's more like a hearty invitation to explore your soul, spark your creativity, and reconnect with the love inside of you. It's a nudge to self-discovery and reflection, an encouragement to shake off the limits that society imposes, and to let yourself expand through growing your own emotional intelligence.

These are things to take on board from a place of safety. Your safety is precious to me. So, before anything else, please practise self-care. Help is only ever a phone call away.

Lovingly
x Lu

Set the Scene

Do your thing, find your space,
Then your thoughts will flow with grace.

Let's set the vibe, my friend – the *sweeeeeeetest* vibe! Whether it's snuggled in your cosy nook, buried in pillows, or soaking up magic in nature, claim your sacred spot. Hydration? Check. Distractions? Handled. Got your favourite pen ready to flow? Excellent.

 Now, let's level it up: light a candle, spritz some sage or your most soothing scent, and, for a final soulful touch, choose your soundtrack. I have curated hours of soul-soothing magic to listen to. No Spotify? Time to download it: trust me, it will be worth it!

Pause...
Feel your
HeART &
bReathe...
1234
inHale → Hold...
1234, Exhale
Repeat

Here are three playlists, which I suggest you play at different moments of this journal:

Focus on Journalling – SYL

Grooves and Creativity – SYL

Medicine Songs for Process – SYL

FOCUS ON JOURNALLING – SYL: These tunes are your secret sauce for dialling in, focusing up, properly pondering, and having your own soul-spilling writing moments. They'll guide you straight to the honest, heartfelt core of you. Crank it up and enjoy the journey!

GROOVES AND CREATIVITY – SYL: This playlist? It's your jam for all things creative! Whether you're colouring outside the lines, vision-boarding your dreams, dancing like no one's watching, or just vibing with the tips, it's here to fuel your fun. Let loose, get random, and boogie whenever the mood strikes. Enjoy, you beautiful, expressive human!

MEDICINE SONGS FOR PROCESS – SYL: This playlist is your companion for those processing moments – when the tears start to rise and the feels are too big to ignore. Pause. Breathe. Be present. Let these tunes hold you and help you to feel it all, and to heal a little more. Love yourself and drench yourself in compassion. You've got this!

Journal and integrate whenever it feels right for you; there are no rules! Whether it's 10 minutes a day, a Sunday afternoon boogie, or scribbling away in the bath on a Wednesday (phone-free, of course!), make it unapologetically *your* time. Cue the perfect playlist, bliss out, and do you – whatever feels right. This is your sacred space to self-nurture. Let the world spin while you ponder, feel, and heal. It's all about *you*. Let's do this. How fun!

Colour in and OUTSIDE the lines

Intentions

Set your sights, make it clear,
Plant your goal and hold it near.

You're here for a reason, whether out of curiosity or because something in you is ready for more. More joy, more love, more you. Let's set the intention that this journey will help you remember how worthy you are, how much light you've got to shine into the world around you. There's no destination in this life, just an unravelling. And this book – *your* book – is here to remind you of that.

♥   *Take a moment to feel into your intention for this journey. What do you hope to gain from it? Remember, we're all figuring it out as we go, so release any pressure and simply tune in to your heart. Free-flow your intention here ...*

Let that intention guide you as you move forward, shaping the unique discoveries and growth that this journal will bring. Setting an intention is powerful – it's about wishing well for yourself, for others, and for every situation you encounter. It's about infusing spaces and moments with your love and wholehearted desire for everything to be revealed in the best possible way. I'm all in for this, and I'm here for it with you. May this journey exceed your hopes, bringing you everything you seek and more for yourself.

A Little About Me

Hello, gorgeous, and welcome.

I'm so grateful you're here ... Thank you for trusting me to help guide you into more exquisite layers of yourself. Let's make a pact to have so much fun while we're doing it – lots of giggles along the way. I want this space to feel like a gorgeous sanctuary where you can fully embrace yourself, in all your shades and colours, and feel supported. I'm delighted you're letting me share empowering and inquisitive words. Every page will help you grow deeper into your emotional intelligence. *Shine Your Light*!

You might be wondering what made me write a book like this? Well, I've lived a wild and messy life. Full of mistakes, healing, love, loss, laughter, and self-doubt. It's been hard, a hoot, and everything in between.

This journal isn't coming from some 'Guru-LuLu, all-knowing sage' place – because, trust me, I'm far from that. When people meet me off the back of watching *Married at First Sight*, I often say, 'I got a good edit!' And it's true – I'm a lot more flawed than what was portrayed on TV. Like you, I'm a work in progress. I'm all about growing as I go – embracing the lessons, staying true to myself, showing up for the ride with open arms, and finding joy in the journey! That's what I want for you, too.

Here I am, pouring my heart into these pages with the hope of profoundly supporting your journey. I believe in the beauty of our shared humanity and the incredible awakening that we're all part of. My intention is to inspire, uplift, and help you navigate life with greater clarity, courage, and connection. At the end of the day, I'm just a woman with an opinion, and I know I won't always get it right. So, take what resonates, leave what doesn't, and let's get into it – perfectly imperfect, side by side.

Emotional intelligence is without a doubt my favourite topic. It's endlessly fascinating, branching out into countless directions that challenge and inspire us to grow in the ways that truly matter. The more we nurture it, the more it nurtures us. Magic!

While I haven't written a PhD on the subject or stacked up degrees, life has been my ultimate teacher. I've given it a good crack – given it my all – stumbled many times, and often spectacularly, but picked myself back up again (haven't we all?). Each misstep became a lesson, and every 'failure' was alchemised into an opportunity to realign with something more 'me'.

I'm a self-confessed earth mumma at heart (say whaaaat?): I just want to wrap everyone up in a big hug and whisper, 'You're doing great. It's all going to be okay – better than okay.' I want the absolute best for you, and my hope is that during this process you'll work through some of your stuff, let go of what no longer serves you, and take a massive leap into more of the magnificent you!

• • •

I had the privilege of growing up in a charming pocket of the state of Victoria: right on the Esplanade in Mornington, with the beach just steps from my door. It was so very Australian! My childhood was a joyful whirlwind of sandy toes, tree-climbing escapades, and wild adventures. My siblings and I spent carefree days pulling silly stunts and laughing until our sides hurt. What a gift those years were!

Of course, it wasn't all sunshine and giggles. There were the inevitable arguments, dreaded chores, and this persistent nagging feeling – like I was somehow out of sync with those around me; like they were all following a path I'd never been able to find. That sense of being slightly offbeat lingered for years, quietly threading itself into the fabric of my story. Even so, the world felt like an endless classroom, and I flung myself into absorbing all its lessons with insatiable curiosity and a love of people from all sorts of backgrounds and cultures.

My tendency was to fall deeply in love, each time for long stretches (a serial monogamist, you could say). By the time I turned 43, I'd experienced seven incredible intimate partnerships – each one unique and a perfect reflection of where I had been in my personal growth at that time. I was on a quest for happiness, taking the winding road to explore every crevice of myself to become (fingers crossed) the best version of me. That was the mission.

No part of this journey has been without emotional turmoil. I'm one of those sensitive souls whose body stores and expresses emotion, and I've had chronic and debilitating back issues over the years. There have been times when the pain has been so intense, perfectly synching with heartbreak, that I've been completely out of action for months. Thank goodness for my mum, who's always been there to hold space and help me piece things back together. I've been blessed beyond to have retreated to Mum's ocean sanctuary when I've needed to rest and recharge. It's my spirit home – the place where my soul truly finds peace. I'm so grateful to have that.

I've spent years chasing extreme experiences, and in many ways that's where I've invested my time and money – into living fully, growing, learning, and stepping into challenges that have pushed me way outside my comfort zone. For almost a year, I travelled in my pop-up van with an outrageously fun lover, soaking up every moment and having the time of my life up and down the East Coast of Australia. Through both work and personal travel, I've been lucky enough to explore a chunk of the globe: England, Ireland, Scotland, Wales, India, Indonesia, Malaysia, Thailand, Singapore, China, Egypt, the US, Canada, Peru, Argentina, Bolivia, Mexico, Cyprus, Italy, France, the Netherlands, Sweden, Hungary, Bosnia, Slovenia, Austria, Croatia, Fiji, and New Zealand.

It's been incredible to have had some long stints living abroad. I've volunteered in less-fortunate places, done a medicine retreat with my sister deep in the Amazon – with the Shipibo tribe – and hunted down the best dancefloors around the world. I've lived in meditation centres and hosted large workshops and retreats on tantra, relationships, lifestyle, and spirituality. I've also been a part of groups like the coastal crew 'The Dodgy Dunkers', who meet near my mum's home every morning at 7, year-round, to be refreshed by the ocean and its healing medicine (honestly, it's the best way to start the day)! Each country, community, and cultural immersion has contributed to shaping me into who I am today.

Appearing on *Married at First Sight Australia*, Series 11, was one of the most outlandish things I've embarked on, and it certainly was a defining chapter. It gave me the chance to open my heart and step into a marriage that was unlike anything I'd experienced before. The entire experiment was a profound eye-opener, filled with unexpected lessons and connections. While I may not have walked away with the husband I'd hoped for, I gained something even greater: a beautiful, global community that continues to surprise and enrich my life in the most wonderful ways.

After *MAFS*, I was amazed at how many people were interested in learning from my emotional intelligence. The demand was so great that I decided to create a subscription-based portal. For a small fee, members could join me twice a month for webinars called 'Ask Lu'. I'd set a topic in advance, and during these sessions members had the chance to ask anything related to it. The connection and curiosity were so palpable!

I named this amazing group of people my 'Tribe', and watching them connect and practise what we were exploring together filled my heart with pride. As the questions kept pouring in, this book began to take shape, blossoming from the 'Ask Lu' sessions and the monthly newsletter I'd been sharing. So, my beautiful Tribe and ever-growing village, this book is a love letter to you and your personal journeys! Thank you for trusting me to be a part of your growth. I've learnt so much through my time with the Tribe, and many of your questions were deeply relatable. With immense respect and gratitude, I've woven some of those questions into this book, as they continue to inspire and guide us.

So, who am I? I'm Lucinda Light – a woman who's walked the winding roads of life, stumbled, gotten back up, and kept moving toward something real. I've shed that old feeling of 'being out of sync' that followed me around for years, sometimes leaving me in a vague haze. I'm really comfy these days embracing the mystery, with all its twists and turns, knowing that every step keeps leading me to exactly where I'm meant to be.

Over the years, I've practised stretching and challenging myself. Countless times, I've walked – all wobbly – into the unknown, undertaking soul-searching, radical self-reflection, owning my mistakes, trying new things and embracing self-acceptance in its rawest form. Recognising my flaws has been a powerful gateway, teaching me that true transformation happens when we honour all of who we are – our strengths and our struggles alike.

I'm here to tell you: as I find my way and shine my light, so will you! Let's illuminate the path ahead together, one step at a time. Get ready to immerse yourself in this journey – you're going to love it! Let's kick things off by defining emotional intelligence – only, you'll have to read it in poetry! Yep, poetry is sprinkled throughout this book because I love rhythm and rhyme. It's my 'Dr. Seuss Loose' side; always ready to have a go at some soul-enriching wordplay!

Say this out Loud I'm FABULOUS say it like you mean it!

Emotional Intelligence

Gorgeous, let's lay the groundwork and dive in deep!
Emotional intelligence – what you sow and practise, you reap!

Keep showing up and journalling – and shine your inner light,
Share your radical truth 'cause there's no wrong or right!

Emotional intelligence is for us all, with so many exquisite jewels,
Learning to attend to our feelings, and oh so many tools.

Understanding and managing your emotions, and others' too,
You'll gain self-awareness and a compassionate view.

Unlike IQ, which is set and fixed in its place,
EI can be nurtured and grown at a progressive pace.

Between emotion and logic, it finds its sweet spot,
It's here for you to evolve – an ability we've all got.

So, here's to the journey, both fun and profound,
With emotional intelligence, let's spread love all around.

I'm delighted you're aboard, 'cause there's so much to share
Put the work in now and your joy will be beyond compare!

Thanks for being here, you wonderful human!
X Lu

Emotions are vast and complex, and it's not always easy to pinpoint what you're feeling. Children start with the basics – happiness, sadness, fear; there are countless more. But learning about emotions is a lifelong process. Emotions continue to be unpredictable and sometimes overwhelming all through adulthood.

We operate in two worlds – our inner world (mind and body) and the outer world. Emotions like joy, fear, or anger are an intricate interplay between these worlds. Seeing a snarling dog, for example, may trigger fear: a racing heart, widened eyes, and the instinct to freeze or flee. It can be handy to think of emotions as data: they give us useful information that helps us know who we are, what we want, and how to make effective decisions about our behaviour.

Cultivating emotional intelligence is about gaining a deeper understanding of your emotions – how they shape your thoughts, influence your body, and drive your behaviour. The aim is simple: rather than suppressing your feelings, allow yourself to fully experience them. This involves tuning in to the emotions of others, understanding how they influence you and, in turn, becoming mindful of the impact you have on them.

• • •

Start right where you're at, using whatever you've got. The further you go, the more you'll grow your awareness, enlarge your toolkit, and fall more in love with who you are – all while cherishing the connections you share with others.

I'm here to guide you, to help you trust in the process, and to encourage you to dive into the richness of your inner world. You're utterly divine! Thank you for exploring these spaces with me. Document your divine evolution as you go – your growth, your big feels, and your cartwheels into becoming the most radiant, sparkling version of yourself. Let's keep painting the most breathtaking emotional landscapes together and planting seeds of magic that will continue to flourish.

KNOW THYSELF

In the vast expanse of the Universe wide,
The one place to improve is where you reside – inside.

From a young age, I unknowingly switched on my emotional intelligence, though I didn't have the vocabulary for it back then. At primary school, most of my friends were naturally gorgeous. I saw myself as the plump kid, sporting braces. Rightly or wrongly, I felt I had to rely on my personality to find my place in this world, so my focus was on being funny, caring, and adaptable. As you can imagine, there was trial and error. Keen to know how it was all landing, I tuned in to other people's emotions.

During high school, I further developed these skills, which became second nature. I was drawn to the 'cool cats' – the ones who were mature for their age – and in building friendships with them, I taught myself to leverage charisma and emotional awareness. This opened doors for me socially. At 19, when I became a tour leader for a small-group adventure enterprise in Asia – the youngest person the company had ever appointed to this position – instinctively, I knew how to meet each person where they were at. I adored the art of group dynamics, and earnt five-star reviews from travellers around the world, year after year. I honed my ability to connect with others, something I've continued to do throughout my many enriching relationships and career changes.

· · ·

Shortly before entering my teenage years, I had a crash course in empathy, adaptability, and working through emotional pain via my parents' difficult divorce. When my cherished family took on a new shape, it felt as if the guiding star that had always lit my way had been torn from the sky. This upheaval thrust me into uncharted territory, forcing me to tap into my resilience, and in ways I had never imagined.

The irony is that I had great stores of resilience because my parents were – and remain – wonderful people who loved my two siblings and me unconditionally. Mum and Dad were not only creative and entrepreneurial – they managed their business and renovated homes with flair – but also unfailingly supportive of us kids, even amid their own personal challenges. In the 80s, when I was growing up – as the third child – our house was a hub of celebrations, filled with laughter, music, and endless joy. Our double-storey beach house was a place of delectable homemade food, cosy fires in winter and in summer fresh ocean breezes. Against a backdrop of glistening sunsets, and to the soundtrack of my dad's vinyl record collection, I grew up feeling proud of where I lived and of my family.

My parents were incredible role models. One of the highlights of my childhood was their creative venture – an old apple cool-store they transformed into an art centre for local craftspeople and makers. The place was a sensory wonderland. It had a signature perfume: the rich earthiness of ageing wood mingling with the scent of dried flowers, the mustiness of old pianola scrolls, and the mouthwatering aroma of hot scones emanating from the tea room. Heavenly.

It was after life threw Mum and Dad a massive challenge, which they reacted to in wholly different ways, that they came undone as a couple. My mum then entered a new relationship; her partner had children too, and so my brother, sister, and I had to share her. Meanwhile, my dad relocated to the city, an hour's drive away; he, too, was suddenly less available to us. At 13, I found an escape from my uncomfortable feelings in substances and reckless weekends, losing myself in a haze of fun and mischief while trying to stay emotionally afloat.

Much of the academic side of school was a slog, but I thrived in drama, literature, and art. These creative realms were where I felt most alive. Socially, I gravitated toward the daring, rebellious kids, and together we caused plenty of harmless trouble: laughing, getting kicked out of class, sneaking into parties, and making memories that I hold dear.

A pivotal moment came at 15, when I stepped away from the crowd and forged a deep, lasting bond with one person. This friendship became one of the cornerstones of my life and, together, my bestie and I set off on a month-long adventure to Indonesia before our final year of school. It was more than just a holiday: it was a transformative experience that ignited our love for travel. After graduating high school, I worked tirelessly in hospitality to fund my next trip. Returning to Bali, I fell head over heels for one of a pair of Balinese twins, while my bestie fell for the other!

This whirlwind romance swept me into thrilling escapades across Indonesia, India, and Malaysia. When the chance to become a tour leader came up, I seized it, basing myself in Thailand. My heart, however, was still in Bali, and I believed our love could endure my wayfaring lifestyle. But when I finally returned, I found that my twin had moved on. I was heartbroken.

My journey has been full of unexpected twists, and turns, including dating a Balinese pop star. Life in Bali took a dark turn when the devastating bombing occurred there, tragically claiming the lives of over 100 Australians. After this shocking event, tourism came to a standstill, understandably, and my work dried up too. That heartbreaking chapter became the catalyst for leaving Asia altogether, relocating to Australia, and falling even deeper in love with someone I believed was my forever.

We shared four-and-a-half years of life together, living in the UK, travelling the world, and building memories that felt timeless. But in a period of real struggle – when our relationship was already on shaky ground – I had an accident that left me temporarily unable to walk on one foot. Overwhelmed by the challenges we faced, my partner decided to focus on his own path, leaving me to navigate life and recovery on my own. Single once again. It was a tough chapter, teaching me resilience in the face of heartbreak and uncertainty.

The experience forced me into a period of profound self-reflection during my physical rehabilitation, pushing me to confront aspects of myself I was yet to explore. As I regained my strength, both physically and emotionally, I felt a shift in my journey. I resumed my travels but this time with a deeper sense of purpose, embarking on a spiritual quest that complemented my adventures. That time of adversity, paired with the inner work it sparked, was a powerful turning point. It reminded me, once again, of the invaluable lessons hidden within life's most challenging moments.

• • •

From that turning point onward, I became bolder. I sold the house I'd bought in my early 20s and invested every last cent into developing myself – mind, body, and soul. Over the next decade, I dedicated myself to growth. I dove into workshops, spent a year studying at a transpersonal school to become a holistic counsellor, and trained as a Kahuna bodywork practitioner. I attended every festival and workshop that sparked my curiosity, all while cultivating meaningful relationships with extraordinary people from all walks of life. My network flourished, and so did I.

Eventually, I opened a couple of healing studios where I had the privilege of helping people release trapped emotions, express themselves openly – sometimes for the first time – and let go of what no longer served them. The combination of my holistic counselling skills with deep bodywork naturally attracted an awesome client base, almost entirely through word of mouth. Those years were incredibly fulfilling – a time of connection, healing, and the profound experience of witnessing firsthand the transformation and personal growth of others.

Somewhere in the mix, I fell deeply in love with a bona-fide genius actuary who had two divine kids I absolutely adored, and still do. That chapter alone could fill a book: it featured escapades to Burning Man, creating cabarets, zipping around on café-racer Triumphs, and just generally living a life of exuberance and creativity.

The catch was that he'd undergone an irreversible vasectomy, and I was firmly in my 'I must have a child' phase, which I experienced as an all-encompassing calling. Despite the deep love we shared, we couldn't bridge that fundamental gap in our story. Walking away was utterly devastating. I lost everything: him, the kids, our home, my business, the life we built together, the dream of having a child with him, and even some of the friendships we had nurtured as a couple. Letting go of that identity was excruciating, and starting over meant moving two hours away, back to my mum's place, to face a stark new reality from ground zero.

I embarked upon the reset, fragile and wobbly, with a back that had literally buckled under the weight of it all, and my mental health was hanging by a thread. But step by step, piece by piece, I rebuilt myself – mind, body, and soul – and found my way forward. I kept flipping the script, reframing things, and, yep, it took a good couple of years. I took shaky steps toward the new me, even though at the time I felt so scared and uncertain.

To help claw my way out of my gut-wrenching loss (it felt like a death at the time), I relocated to Byron Bay at the start of the Covid pandemic. My self-reinvention included becoming a registered celebrant and moving into a dreamy beach house with four women. That chapter was healing, intense, and a crash course in communication with all types of personalities. I stayed there for four years, growing and grounding, and sometimes being on my knees begging the universe for a break and a really defining line to my purpose. And then, well, TV came calling. Next thing I knew, I was saying 'I do' to a stranger on *Married at First Sight*. And, well, the rest is history!

Looking back, I see how essential it was to truly know myself – a journey that never ends but one that I've embraced wholeheartedly and prioritised. Emotional intelligence equips us with the tools to navigate life with greater clarity, deepen self-love, and embolden us to reach for more. Life is a teacher, no doubt, but, wow, asking the right questions? That's where you can hasten the process. And in this book, this is what I am offering you: a lot of questions to prompt your own soul-searching.

Who Are You?

Are you the sum of your choices or the voice in your head,
When you're brushing your teeth or lying in bed?
Are you your quirks, your dreams, your regrets?
Or the talents you've got that no one forgets?

In this section of your journal, I want you to jot down the things you know for sure about yourself. Recognising what makes you *you* is seriously powerful. For example, at my core, I'm creative, a nature lover, a bit of a loner. I know, right? You probably didn't see that coming, but it is true: scout's honour – and I'm a massive homebody. Yet flip the switch and I'm an absolute party animal! I'm a true ambivert. I value family, my soul tribe, adventure, generosity, joy, fun, beauty, and a life that's always evolving.

I love revisiting the reflections below because, as we grow, so do our self-perceptions and desires. They will change a bunch through your life. Go grab that pen of yours and chase what truly lights you up!

What are your core traits and values?

♥ *How do your values play out in your everyday life? Whether it's kindness, honesty, or creativity, how do these guide your actions and interactions?*

♥ *What lights you up? The activities and interests that make you feel most alive – those are your gems.*

♥   Time to give yourself some credit. What skills, talents, and unique gifts do you bring to the table that make you you?

♥   What truly sets your soul on fire? Reflect on what drives you and the impact you want to leave behind. Whether it's as a parent, a leader, or a creator, what's your bigger mission?

♥ *Picture your perfect surroundings. Is it a serene nature spot, a bustling city, or a cosy, intimate space? What kind of physical, emotional, or social environment brings out the best in you?*

♥ *What beliefs, mantras, or philosophies guide you through life? What's the focus in times of uncertainty?*

♥ What chapter are you in right now? Reflect on your focus, challenges, and where you're placing your energy.

♥ How do you express yourself through what you wear, how you talk, or how you move? Are you bold and daring or laid back and grounded? Your style says a lot about your inner world.

♥ *Who are the people who nourish and support you? Whether it's family, friends, mentors, or even virtual communities, reflect on how your people shape your life and your identity.*

♥ *Is it a person, a place, or a particular routine? What gives you that sense of peace and belonging, where you feel most grounded in who you are?*

♥ *Take a moment to look at all these details you've unpacked about yourself. Embrace the diversity and complexity of who you are. Reflect on the connections between different aspects of yourself and how they contribute to your unique identity.*

Get cReaTive HeRe...

• • •

You're a beautifully intricate riddle, a wondrous blend of contradictions and dualities. The most captivating individuals embrace their layers, finding joy in their depth and contrasts. I see you, and there's so much more within you waiting to be expressed. Let it flow – enjoy all that makes you uniquely you!

Self-awareness

*Self-awareness is foundational to your emotional intelligence, it lets you
see yourself clearly, care for yourself well, and move with purpose!*

Self-awareness starts with getting curious about your thoughts and feelings. But
it can be a slippery thing, can't it? Just when you think you've nailed it, it wiggles
away! One moment, you're feeling totally in tune with your inner world – your
behaviours, habits, and choices – and the next, a sneaky blind spot knocks you
sideways. Yikes! Take overindulging in food, for instance (guilty as charged!).
You know it's not the best choice, but breaking the habit of being gluttonous?
That's a whole other ball game.

 Lately, with all the touring I've been doing, I've been staying in some
really nice hotels. Put me in front of a breakfast buffet, and suddenly my inner
hunter-gatherer goes into overdrive. Croissants, full English, fruit, a bit of
everything – it's like I've convinced myself it's a survival tactic! And that's where
the gap shows up: the frustrating space between knowing better and actually
doing better.

 But let's be real: it's not just about food. That gap exists emotionally, too.
Whether it's holding on to a grudge longer than we should, reacting when we
should pause, or struggling to let go of habits that don't serve us, we've all felt it.
It's a practice, and while it can be hard, it's also where growth lives.

 Self-awareness helps you step back from impulsive reactions, allowing
you to respond with more thoughtfulness and empathy, which in turn fosters
stronger relationships. I often remind myself, 'Check yourself, Lu!' because self-
awareness is something we need to return to again and again – it's a lifelong
practice, not a one-time fix.

 There's so much to explore about this absolute foundation of emotional
intelligence, so let's work together to illuminate more awareness within you.

 Respond in the space provided or feel free to shimmy on out onto an extra
page, you fabulously wondrous human:

♥ When do you feel most like yourself? With what humans? A family member, a friend, a stranger? Reflect on moments when you feel authentic and true to your core.

♥ What is weighing you down the most in your life right now? Describe your emotional, mental, or physical burdens.

♥ *Recognise your strengths. Don't be shy – list them here and get really clear.*

♥ *Recognise your weaknesses. Don't be too harsh on your good self!*
Things like: I'm a bit disorganised, I'm a bit awkward socially ...

Self-awareness isn't just about knowing yourself – it's also about understanding how your emotions, habits, and actions affect the people around you. How do you think your behaviour and attitude lands with strangers that you have brief encounters with? How about your loved ones?

• • •

Self-awareness is your personal power – an anchor in a chaotic world. It brings clarity to the way you move through life, your emotions and choices – inviting you to pause, reflect, and evolve. By truly seeing yourself, you open the door to possible transformation. In three months from now, 'future you' might answer some of the above questions differently. Isn't that intoxicating!

Confidence

Confidence blooms from the courage to dare,
For every step forward, you strengthen your flair. Yeah!

Confidence-building is something you gotta work at consistently. If you're already rocking that confident AF energy, strut on over to another entry, you radiant gem – and good on you! And for those of you that don't feel that way – I want you to know it's okay if you're still finding your footing; you will get there.

People often tell me how confident I seem, but what they don't see is how hard and how often I push myself to step outside my comfort zone – feeling rather wobbly while I do it. 'Courage over comfort' – the catchcry of author Brené Brown – is a phrase that I deeply jam with. So, once in a while, I take a leap of faith, thrust myself outside of my comfort zone – whether it's sharing my thoughts in a meeting, divulging new stories on stage, being outrageous with my clothes choices on TV, or simply being vulnerable.

Even if there is the odd stumble, sure enough, I feel my confidence strengthen. It's like building a muscle: the more I flex it, the more confident I become. I still get nervous, but I've learnt that those feelings are just part of the process. These days, I've reframed the visceral feeling of nerves to 'expansion'. I've had to.

Finding your confidence involves embracing those awkward moments (what I call my awks and dorks!), learning to trust yourself, and recognising that it's perfectly normal to feel uncertain occasionally. Every step you take outside of what feels familiar helps you grow and discover that the world isn't as intimidating as it seems. Remember, confidence doesn't mean the absence of fear; it means choosing to act in spite of it.

So, I invite you to explore your own stratosphere. What small steps can you take today that will stretch and grow your confidence? How can you celebrate your progress, no matter how small that forward momentum may be? Embrace your unique path, and trust that you have the strength within you to shimmy shine and overflow with it. You've got this!

Rebuilding lost confidence

When it feels like confidence has 'left the building', it's useful to recognise that this is a natural part of the emotional journey. Confidence can ebb and flow, especially in challenging times. Acknowledging this can be the first step toward regaining it. Here are some simple ways to boost and nurture your confidence:

♥   *Revisit your past achievements for a confidence boost. What past accomplishment reminds you of your strengths?*

♥   *Spend a few minutes daily imagining yourself succeeding in a small future task. How can you bring that vision into your life today?*

♥   *Break tasks into manageable steps and celebrate small victories. What goal can you set today?*

♥   *Trusted friends can highlight strengths you might miss. What strengths do others see in you?*

♥ *Exercise, creativity, or nature lifts your self-esteem. What activity makes you feel most confident?*

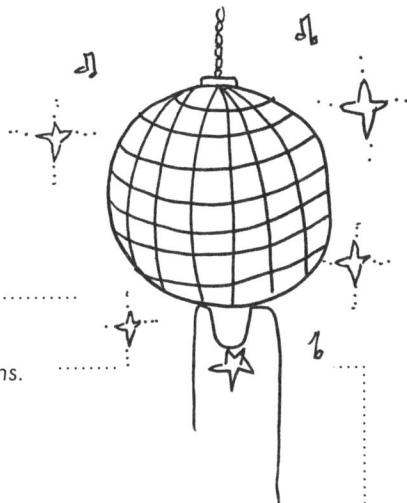

♥ *Replace doubt with empowering affirmations. How can you reframe a negative thought?*

♥ *Celebrate your progress. What unique qualities can you appreciate today?*

♥ *Be as kind to yourself as you would to a friend. How can you be kinder to yourself?*

• • •

Remember, confidence isn't about being flawless: it's about showing up, daring to try, and owning every sparkle and stumble along the way. So, crank up the volume on your inner anthem, let your divine light shine like the one-of-a-kind disco ball you are, and boogie through life like no one's watching (but secretly, everyone's inspired).

Stagnation

When stagnation whispers, 'Stay', let curiosity reply, 'Grow'.
Roots deepen in stillness, but then wings form when you let go.

A friend recently confided in me, saying, 'I feel so stuck. I don't know what to do with my life. It's confusing, it's exhausting, and I just don't know how to move forward.' My heart ached for them because I've been there, too – more times than I'd like to admit. Feeling stuck is one of the toughest emotional spaces to be in. It's like standing at a crossroads and feeling completely disconnected from your true self, not knowing what way to go. And it's staggeringly uncomfortable to be in this state because it challenges every part of us.

Yet, it's also a call to pause, reflect, and recalibrate – a moment that holds the potential for transformation. What feels like stagnation may actually be the stillness before a breakthrough, the space where clarity starts to form. It's often the very discomfort of feeling stuck that drives you to seek change. That ache can push you to question what's not working, envision who you want to become, and find the momentum to move forward once again.

In those moments when I've asked myself, 'What in the bejesus am I doing with my life?' only to come up with nothing but silence and the (fortunately lovely) mating song of crickets, all I craved was for someone to *hand me* the answers – a roadmap or a golden key to my future. I leant on friends, my parents, and professionals, hoping they'd point the way when I couldn't see it. Can you relate? Ekkk.

Here's some good things to ask yourself when you feel stuck and stagnant:

♥ *What specifically makes you feel stuck right now?*

♥ *How does this feeling show up in your daily life?*
Are there noticeable patterns?

♥ *When was the last time you felt truly excited or passionate*
about something?

♥ *What was it?*

♥ *If you could wake up tomorrow living your ideal life, what would it look like?*

♥ *Are there fears or doubts stopping you from pursuing what you truly want?*

♥ *Do you hold any limiting beliefs about yourself? If so, what are they?*

♥ Is there anything else holding you back from moving forward?

♥ What advice would you give someone else if they were in your situation?

♥ What would make you feel proud of yourself five years from now?
What steps can you take to get there?

Find your direction

If you want to soar, release the weight that's been holding you down. It's never too late to dig deep and uncover what's ready to be let go of (oh, the freedom that awaits)! Once that's accomplished, don't get lost up there among the clouds. The following questions will help you settle on a destination before you take to the sky.

♥ *What are the top three values guiding your decisions, and how do your current goals reflect them? Could this be a good time to adjust those goals?*

-

-

-

♥ *Who in your network inspires you – who do you admire – and how can you connect with them more intentionally for guidance?*

♥ *What opportunity will you commit to in the next month that might clarify your path?*

♥ *What new hobby or activity will you explore this month that might help to determine your life direction?*

♥ *What could your life look like this time next year, and what three steps can you take today to move toward that vision?*

-

-

-

♥ *What recent changes have you experienced, and how can you see them as stepping stones toward your new direction?*

• • •

Stagnation is just a pause, not a permanent state. Trust that even in stillness, there's growth happening beneath the surface. The path forward may not always be clear, but the beauty lies in the willingness to step into motion again, understanding that every moment holds the possibility for reinvention. It's never too late to reignite your spark – your next chapter is about to begin, and it's time to step into the light once more.

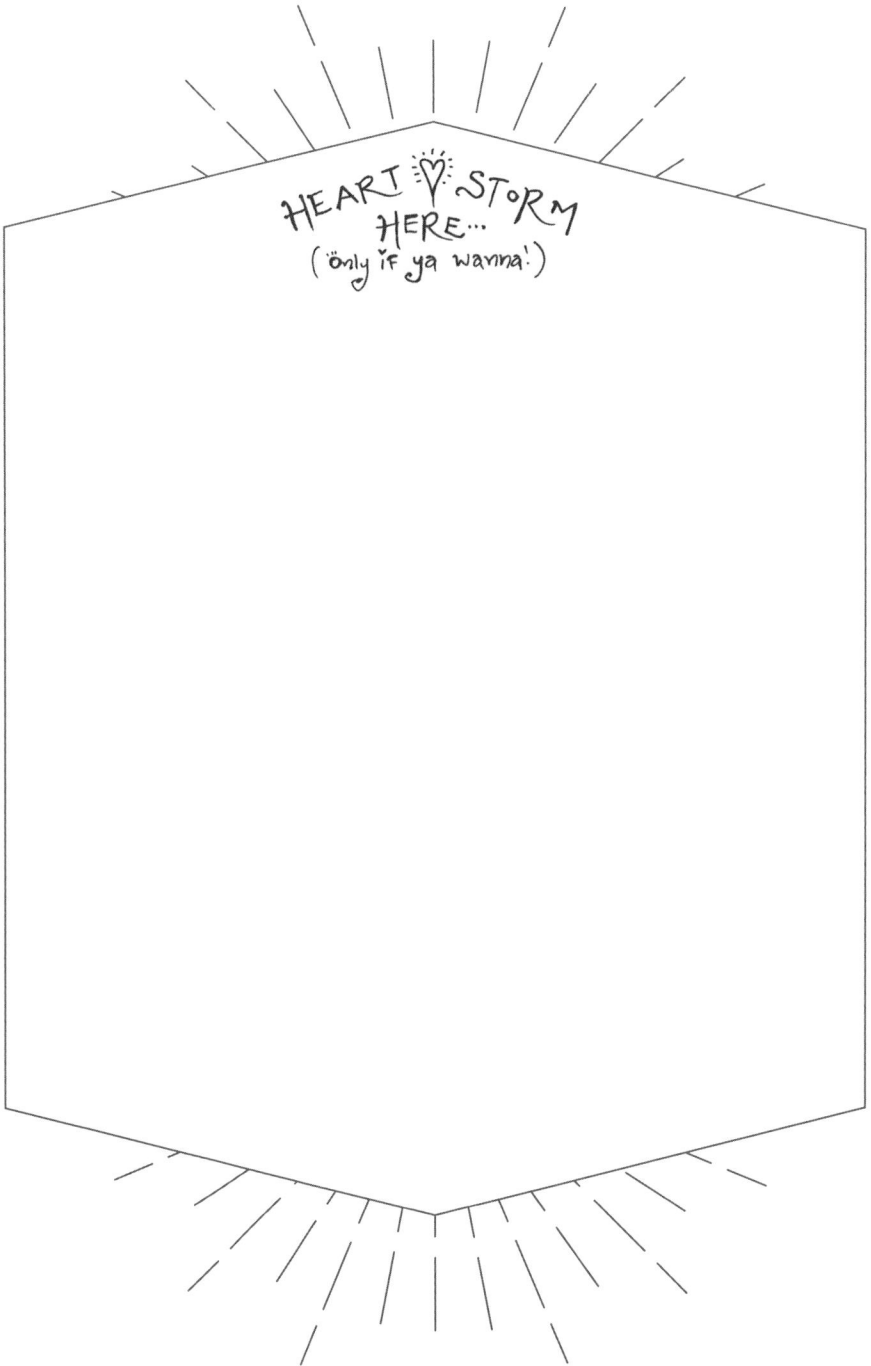

HEART ♥ STORM
HERE...
(önly if ya wanna!)

Lu,

I've just turned 20 and I'm feeling a little lost. What would you tell your 20-year-old self?

Dear Lu,

Take a deep breath and let go. Relax into the rhythm of your life and enjoy the ride – it's meant to be savoured. Follow the sparks that light your heart and let them guide you. Curious about kitesurfing? Go for it! Feeling drawn to conscious relationships? Dive into the best books, podcasts, or workshops you can find. These are your years to explore, to fill your heart with new experiences, to meet extraordinary people, and to follow whatever ignites your soul. Passion will find you naturally when you follow what excites you.

This is your time to gather tools, take bold risks, and live with open-hearted curiosity. Don't take life too seriously. Laugh at the messes and keep showing up for the beauty. You are radiant – don't let self-doubt block your light. Step out of your own way and embrace this messy and magnificent journey.

When fear or worry whispers in your ear, pause. Look for the good, no matter how small, and let gratitude anchor you. Hold onto the mantras that keep you steady, like, 'Life is always working out for me.' Don't just say it: feel it in your bones. Believe in the magic of that truth.

Keep writing these letters, Lu. They're a gift to yourself. They ground you, remind you, and help you to call in the future you're dreaming of. It will all come true, I promise, you will become the full, blooming Lucinda you dream of. It's happening even now, with every step you take. Keep calling her in. Be your biggest cheerleader. Be kind to yourself, be proud of yourself, and stay soft, kind, and open – even when life throws you a curveball or three.

When things feel hard, let yourself feel it all – get the support you need, learn from the pain, and then let it go. These moments will build your resilience, but don't let them hold you hostage. You're too vibrant for that, Lu. When you feel consumed by grief, adversity, pain – the feel it all but keep tractioning forward in your healing, don't get stuck there.

Surround yourself with people who lift you up and see your light. When the weight of the world feels heavy, go outside. Breathe deeply. Let nature remind you of your place in the bigger picture. You are so loved, more than you can imagine. And I'm endlessly grateful for you – just as you are.

With all the love in the world,
X Lu

Writing to myself – both my younger self and for that young woman – was an incredibly beautiful experience. It gave me goosebumps and filled me with awe and deep gratitude for everything I've been through and how far I've come. To every 20-something who feels a bit lost, I want to shout from the mountaintops: You are divine! Life has your back, and you've got your own. Just keep showing up!

You are a radiant, exquisite spark of the Universe. Know it, feel it, own it in every inch of your being. Thank you, from the depths of my heart, for being here, for choosing growth, for seeking something deeper than the fleeting pursuit of external beauty (although, enjoy that too!).

It all begins within. That light, that power, that truth – it's all within you. Discovering more of yourself is the most enriching adventure you can ever embark on.

• • •

Oh, to be 20-something again! But honestly, I have to say ... the 40s are shaping up to be my favourite decade so far! I feel so blessed and grateful to say that. There's something truly freeing about feeling at peace in my own skin, owning who I am unapologetically.

I wish this same peace and joy for you – no matter your age or where you are in life. May all beings be happy; may all beings be well. We're here to thrive!

Stress Less

Too blessed to be stressed!
Now, that's a good thing to say often to your gorgeous self!

During spikes of inner turmoil or external-world clamour, our body – and mind – experiences feelings of tension, aka stress. While not exactly pleasant, stress is an inevitable part of life – a signal that we're stretching, growing, or simply wading through the complex demands of being human. Stress can hum in the background of our mind when the clock's ticking too fast; it can roar during high-pressure moments, or even spill out from the energy of others around us. But here's the truth: stress doesn't have to overwhelm you. With the right tools, it can become a doorway to deeper self-awareness and growth.

Stress has an uncanny way of shining a spotlight on what's not working. Some of my most overwhelming physical experiences have been my body's clear message: *This pace? This situation? It's not sustainable.* Those moments forced me to stop, reassess, and reimagine how I navigate life's pressures. Managing stress isn't just about finding quick relief; it's about building a meaningful and respectful relationship with yourself, where you can really listen to your needs.

For me, stress has been a catalyst for learning when to pause, take a deep breath, and honour my boundaries. How about you? Turning to practices like mindful breathing, immersing yourself in nature, or carving out moments of stillness isn't just coping, it's self-respect in action. These small, intentional acts remind us that our wellbeing matters, and to take extra care when things become chaotic. The more we nurture these habits, the more grounded, resilient, and responsive we'll feel. Here are some emotionally intelligent strategies and questions to ponder for lowering stress:

♥   When stress arises, can you shift your perspective from OMG! or (perhaps) negative self-talk to seeing it as a message – then investigating what it might be telling you? What's one way you can reframe your usual stress-response thoughts with self-compassion?

♥   When stress hits, how often do you pause to focus on your breath? How could making this a regular practice change your stress response?

♥ *What other mindful practices can you use to stay in the moment when stress pulls you elsewhere? Go on, list 'em! Look to mindfulness, movement, or nature walks.*

♥ *How comfortable are you with saying 'no'? What steps can you take to better honour your limits?*

♥   What's one recurring source of stress in your life, and how might you begin to address it with curiosity and compassion?

♥   How can you show yourself the same compassion you'd offer a friend going through a stressful time?

♥ *Who can you reach out to when you need to talk? How can their support help lighten your stress?*

♥ *Put your social observation hat on. How does stress present in your loved ones?*

♥   When stress inevitably builds up, how can you inject humour or playfulness to lighten the mood?

♥   What three things can you be grateful for today to shift your perspective? There's opportunities all over this journal to sing praises ...

-

-

-

• • •

Remember that each moment of tension and stress is an opportunity to listen, adjust, and grow. When you stop running and start tuning in, you'll find that stress doesn't have to be the villain, but rather a guide – one that leads you to a more balanced, intentional way of living. Embrace the pauses, honour your limits, and trust that by respecting your own needs, you're paving the path to deeper resilience. Keep breathing, keep listening, and keep trusting the process: your best self is waiting to emerge.

Play

Play is nature's reset button – boosting your mood, sparking your creativity, and sneaking in health benefits while you're busy having fun!

When I was brainstorming with friends and writing my one-woman show, 'An Evening with Lucinda Light', I kept asking myself, 'What has truly helped me thrive emotionally?' To my surprise, play topped the list. Why the surprise? I guess it's easy to underestimate the magic that play unlocks. Play cuts through tension, breaks toxic energy, and brings connection, laughter, and joy. Children are our greatest teachers in this – they live fully in the present, effortlessly releasing stress and worry.

Whether it's being carefree, silly, or a little nonsensical, dancing through life, partying, or laughing at the cosmic joke, play has always been a key part of my wellbeing. Do you play lots in your life? How good is it! During my *Married at First Sight* experience, I found some fun characters to play with who made me laugh through the madness. I'm not sure I would've made it through without willing playmates. Writing about play in my show felt incredibly joyful and true, and I am excited to share its importance here in your emotional intelligence toolkit.

I believe play is your natural birthright, not something to be forgotten. It's a simple yet powerful way to express feelings and lighten life's load – don't you think? I want you to be really playful with this chapter and rip it up a bit, stick weird and random silly things in it, play outside the box. I want you to be as cheeky and as playful as you can be – always with a commitment to doing no harm. Give yourself full permission to play!

♥   When was the last time you truly let go and played like a child? How did it make you feel?

♥   What's your favourite playful activity that instantly lifts your mood, no matter how old you are?

♥   How does play show up in your daily life – whether it's through humour, creativity, or spontaneity?

♥ Have you ever noticed how laughter can instantly shift the energy in a room? What's the last thing that made you laugh uncontrollably?

♥ Can you think of a time when play helped you process a difficult emotion or situation?

More play in ya day!

Here's a list of lighthearted play ideas to bring some cheeky fun and energy into your family, friendship group, or workplace settings and switch things up somewhat:

Silly hat day. Everyone wears the goofiest hat they can find for the day. Bonus points for creativity!

Dance break. Set a timer for a spontaneous five-minute dance party. Let loose and shake off any seriousness!

Compliment balloons. Write compliments on balloons or bury them in the balloon and fling them around the space so folk can read them and be filled with joy. Starter ideas: You're my jam! You're a hunk of spunk! How dare you be so gorgeous!

Funny face contest. Take it in turns and see who can make the funniest face. Snap pictures for a fun 'wall of fame'.

Office/Family Olympics. Create silly challenges (like chair races or paper aeroplane flying) and award medals to the winners.

Pet rock decorating. Everyone gets a stone that can sit in the palm of their hand, paints it and gives it a quirky name. Display finished pet rocks proudly!

Role reversal. Have everyone switch roles for an hour. Managers can be assistants; kids can act like parents ... hilarity will ensue!

Improv story circle. Each person adds a sentence to a story, but they have to use a silly voice. See how ridiculous it gets!

Photo caption contest. Share funny or awkward photos and have everyone create the best caption. Vote on the funniest one!

Mystery lunch swap. Everybody brings a packed lunch – something inventive (omg: better list any allergens on the packaging!). They all go in a pile and everyone chooses. Enjoy the surprise and share laughs over unusual food pairings!

Pillow talk. For a meeting or family gathering, everyone brings their pillow. The idea is to share their funniest or most embarrassing moments while lying on their pillow and chatting horizontally – eye to eye.

Silly sock day. Everyone wears the wackiest socks they can find. Have a 'sock runway' to show them off!

Post-It note challenge. Write funny or inspirational notes and stick them around the workplace or home for others to find throughout the day.

'What's in the box?' game. Fill a box with random household items (nothing sharp, though, darling heart). Blindfolded participants have to guess what's inside by feeling it!

Emotion charades with a twist. Instead of acting out movies and having everyone guess them, act out complex emotions like 'sassy joy' or 'calm determination'. After each emotion has been guessed, the group discusses how to express it in daily life.

• • •

Did you know play is a powerhouse hack for adulting? It's like a secret weapon for your brain – boosting neuroplasticity, keeping you sharp, and making you flexible and fun. Laugh, be spontaneous, be silly! Play slashes stress, builds emotional resilience, and strengthens connections. It's your natural antidote to burnout and overload. So, honey heart, play isn't just for kids: level up and play more; do it for your mental and emotional wellbeing! The world needs your playful twinkle more than ever! Boom shakalaka!

Positivity

When you shift to a positive view, the world transforms,
The things you see take on new forms.

I'm so excited to share with you some ways to bring positivity to your party. People often ask how I stay so upbeat, and I owe a lot of it to my parents, who are natural optimists and modelled that mindset for me. The mantra of my dad (aka 'Pimp Daddy') is 'Seize the day and take no prisoners'. Meaning: live fully in the present and savour the moment, and don't bring along anyone who isn't aligned with that path.

Even with a solid foundation like that, I'll admit I've taken some detours down 'Negative Nancy Avenue' now and then. Not to mention that life doesn't always go smoothly. The key is to recognise what's happening and not get pulled into lingering negativity.

On the other hand, let's be mindful not to fall into the trap of toxic positivity – the belief that we must ignore our reality and just stay positive no matter what. Instead, I believe in accepting life as it is, finding lessons and wisdom in every experience, even the tough ones. We need to embrace the hard moments, allowing ourselves to fully process them. Let's not forget, you've got to 'feel to heal'. In time, things that seemed like hurdles can transform into sparks of light and growth.

Each challenge can be an invitation for growth and transformation. So, stay flexible and open to the kindness life has to offer, and remember, when you radiate positivity, that energy often finds its way back to you tenfold. Here are some uplifting reflections and tips to help you on this journey.

Consistent choices

Positivity is a succession of choices. Surround yourself with positive experiences, uplifting people, and situations that light you up. Be mindful of what you consume – whether it's media, books, or music, everything is frequency and energy. What you focus on expands, so choose to focus on the good stuff.

♥   *What are three positive experiences, people, or activities that you can consciously and consistently choose to include in your life this week to uplift your energy?*

-

-

-

Clearing internal debris

Regularly engage in introspection and emotional clearing. This might involve journalling, talking with a trusted friend or therapist, or simply allowing yourself to process and release any lingering negativity. Clearing internal debris opens up space for positivity to flourish.

♥   *How will you create space for positivity in your life through introspection or conversation, and when do you commit to doing it? Come up with three ideas to clear out your internal debris.*

-

-

-

Free Flow Here...

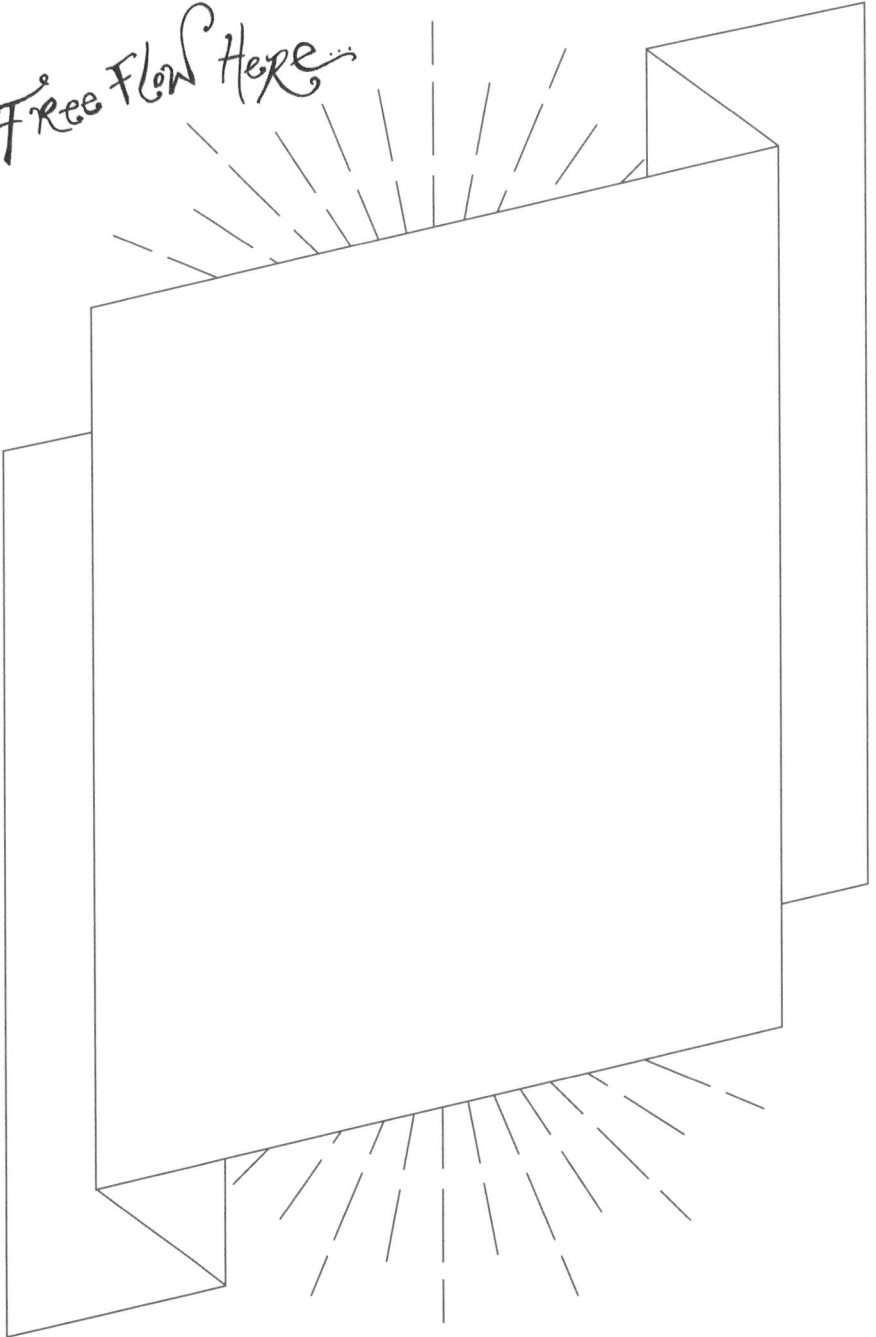

Celebrate small wins

Acknowledge and celebrate small victories each day. This practice reinforces a positive mindset and helps you stay motivated. Be kind to yourself and take it one day at a time. You're doing great!

♥   *What are three small wins you achieved this week, and how will you celebrate this to reinforce your positive mindset and motivation?*

-
-
-

Reframe and flip the script
[Drumroll please: this is my secret sauce!]

Life can serve up some incredible plot twists, but here's the challenge: when things get messy, can you flip the script? Instead of letting a crappy situation define you, try reframing it into something that fuels your growth or brings clarity. This has been my go-to for tractioning forward and remaining a somewhat positive person.

Reframing isn't about denying the tough stuff; it's about choosing to see the lesson, the silver lining, or even just a way forward. For example:

- Got rejected? What if it's clearing space for something better?
- Made a mistake? What if it's the exact experience you needed to level up?
- Feeling stuck? What if this pause is a chance to reassess and recharge?

♥ *Take a situation in your life that feels heavy and flip it into something that sparks hope or action. You've got the power to rewrite the narrative, so take the pen – literally and figuratively – and make it a damn good story:*

- The situation:
- The reframe:
- Your new focus:

. . .

Positivity isn't about chasing perfection; it's about embracing the full spectrum of life and letting every experience, whether smooth or stormy, shape you into someone wiser and more luminous. Let positivity amplify your radiance, using both light and shadow to add depth and richness to your story. Each time you choose gratitude over grumbling, hope over hassle, you strengthen your resilience and refill your positivity well. So, celebrate the little win and revel in the messy brilliance of being human, and keep shining with your one-of-a-kind glow. Make the effort to be unapologetically and gloriously fuelled by positivity! (At least most of the time ...!)

Positive Affirmations

Positive affirmations and nurturing self-talk are among the great keys to elevating your confidence and self-worth. There have been times in my life where I was hugely self-doubting and, for a while there, my home was littered with Post-It notes of positivity to help recode my noggin. While it might feel unfamiliar at first, this practice is deeply empowering and cleansing.

Even in challenging moments, affirmations can positively influence your subconscious, guiding you towards a more self-assured you. Stick them on the bathroom mirror, in your wallet, or as reminders that pop up on your calendar or alarm. Leave some in the pockets of your favourite jackets, or get your best mates to remind you of them. Keep them close and keep re-reminding yourself of all you need to know. Use affirmations that work for your life. You've got this!

POSITIVE AFFIRMATIONS, LET'S GO!

'I am capable, strong, and worthy of love.'

'I embrace my imperfections and appreciate my unique qualities.'

'I radiate positivity and attract abundance into my life.'

♥   *Choose one of the above, or think of a more personal affirmation you would like to try.*
Write it out and stick it on your bathroom mirror to reinforce this encouragement daily. Once the medicine has done its work, try another one that feels appropriate.

POSITIVE AFFIRMATION IDEAS FOR THE CREATIVES AMONG US

As I write this book, one of my dear friends is on a life-altering journey with cancer. She's facing it head on like an absolute warrior. She's come up with creative ways to sneak in affirmations throughout the day, regularly checking in with herself to stay grounded and positive as she battles this challenge.

♥   *See if any of these spark ideas for you!*

Jar
Write down your favourite affirmations on colourful slips of paper, fold them up, and toss them in a jar. Each day, pull one out and let it guide your mindset.

Stones
Write affirmations on small stones or pebbles using a permanent marker. Keep them in your pocket, in the garden, or on your desk as little reminders of your strength.

Playlist
Create a playlist of songs that inspire you. Or take inspiration from the Medicine Songs for Process playlist that I have made for you. Play it when you need it.

Coasters
Write affirmations on coasters that you can use at home or work. Each time you take a sip, you'll be reminded of your positive mindset.

• • •

Affirmations are like your brain's personal hype squad – complete with pom poms, love-heart emojis, and glitter! Seriously, it's like telling your inner critic to take a back seat while your inner cheerleader does a double backflip. Every time you repeat an affirmation, you're basically giving your self-doubt a firm, 'Not today, friend!' Say after me, 'I'm fabulous!' Now say it again! ... Yes, you are!

Negative Patterns

Be gone, Negative Nancy patterns, be gone!

Life has a way of throwing the same lessons at you until you finally face them head on, don't you find? Those negative patterns that hold you back – they're frustratingly persistent. And, I'll be honest: I'm still battling a few of my own. One of my biggest? The constant loop of negative self-talk about my weight. Been dragging round the old 'fatty boom boom' story for years, and even though I know better, it still sneaks up on me and back-chats my reflection on occasion.

Letting go of long-held self-limiting beliefs and patterns of behaviour isn't easy – it's messy, uncomfortable, and sometimes it feels impossible. But while the work is hard – made harder because our brain is wired to make us stick with what it knows – it's definitely worth it. I've learnt that acknowledging the patterns is the first step. Every time I catch myself spiralling into that old mindset, I can say, 'Not today, body-shamer', then I remind myself that I don't need to carry this weight anymore (pardon the pun). Cue the internal cheer squad! You, too, can ditch your sticky negative self-talk – we're in this together!

There's another tricky category of 'nego' patterns: the ones we're not proud of and would rather keep hidden. I'm talking about reactions that don't show us in a good light, beliefs that are totally illogical yet continue to weigh us down (pardon that weighty pun again!), or habits that don't align with who we truly want to be. Here's the good news: we're not permanently stuck. These patterns aren't your destiny (or mine); they're just well-worn grooves in our story. You've got your pen in full swing now, so it's time to rewrite the narrative!

This entry is your call to action. Let's delve into the beauty of flushing out negative patterns, replacing them with new positive codes and power moves. YeeeHaaaaa ... warrior one yoga stance ahoy!

♥   Is there a recurring negative pattern in your life that you know is holding you back? If so, how does it show up in your daily thoughts or actions?

♥   When was the last time you caught yourself spiralling into an old, unhelpful mindset? What could you do differently next time to stop the cycle?

♥ What beliefs or habits are you holding onto simply out of comfort, despite knowing they don't align with the person you aspire to be?

♥ How would it feel to release the weight of those old stories that no longer serve you? What might be possible if you let them go?

♥ *What new empowering pattern would you like to create for yourself, and what's one small action you can take today to start building it?*

Notes and Stuff...

The ritual of release

I love an opportunity for a ritual, being a celebrant and all that! Let's make this powerful. Grab a fresh piece of paper that's not attached to this journal and pour your shadows out onto it – in whatever way you choose – all your fears, negative patterns, and limiting beliefs. When you're done, safely destroy it: tear it up, burn it, or shred it like you mean it while holding in your heart and head this mantra: 'It is done, it is done, it is done.' Watch it go and feel the freedom of releasing what no longer serves you.

• • •

Letting go of the negative patterns is like decluttering your emotional closet. Chances are, you will uncover a few cringeworthy relics (hello, questionable 90s knitted sweater). Once they're gone, you've made room for something fabulous. It's time to toss that 'negative' emotional baggage, step boldly into your light, and reclaim your radiance. You're unstoppable!

Vulnerability

Soft as morning light,
unmasking shadows within,
hearts speak without fear.
Openness unfolds,
quiet strength in being seen,
fragile yet so free.

Vulnerability is about shedding the armour and letting others see you for who you truly are – your fears, your insecurities, your creative sparks, and, yes, even your weaknesses. It's the courage to be fully seen, no filters, and in doing so it deepens connections and creates space for real, authentic relationships. I deeply value embracing vulnerability with my closest circle, finding strength and connection in those authentic moments. I also lean into it when sharing myself with the world through doing live shows, TV, and even writing this book. Braving new things fuels my creativity.

My beautiful mum has seen me through every stage of my journey – whether I'm on the cusp of a new dream or wrapped in a messy, tear-soaked moment of heartbreak. Bless this mess! I wear my heart on my sleeve, and I'm not afraid to go deep, to really go there. I've found that when I'm open, it invites others to do the same. Call it oversharing, if you want, but to me being real is one of my greatest strengths (at the right time, of course, because it's not always appropriate).

Being on *Married at First Sight* brought its fair share of vulnerable moments, including when watching it back with the rest of the world. At times, I wanted nothing more than to hide under a blanket and avoid the screen entirely. Every angle of me was on display (and, oh, how I wish someone had introduced me to purple shampoo before filming!).

During the process itself, and faced with the sting of rejection, I felt especially raw and vulnerable. Thoughts like *Am I attractive enough?* or *What part of me isn't worth the risk?* crept in, challenging my confidence.

But instead of letting those doubts consume me, I embraced the vulnerability, reminded myself not to take it personally, and offered the space compassion. Ultimately, I had to make peace with what was, embrace the lessons, lean into 'self-romancing', and keep moving forward.

Life is filled with moments that leave you feeling vulnerable – when you're not chosen, when the job slips through your fingers, or when you lose someone dear and your world feels unsteady. These tender, uncertain times call for gentle reflection, a space to feel, acknowledge, and express what's stirring within. Let's approach these moments with care and curiosity. Here's a guiding hand to help you navigate them:

♥ *When do you let yourself be vulnerable? How do you feel afterward? Do you feel empowered, relieved, or maybe even exposed? And, more importantly, how can you use these emotions as cues for your personal growth?*

♥ *What would it look like if you stepped it up – allowed yourself more often to be truly seen, with all your fears, dreams, and messy moments?*

♥ *Are there areas of vulnerability in your life you are withholding? What could opening up in those spaces teach you about yourself and the people you're closest to?*

♥   What are the potential rewards of embracing more vulnerability in your relationships? How might it deepen the emotional connections you share with the people you care about most?

♥   How can you create a safe space for others to be vulnerable without judgement? What does/would it look like for you to model emotional maturity in these moments, and how does/would that affect those around you?

• • •

The rewards of vulnerability aren't always immediate or comfortable, but the richness it brings to your connections and to your own growth is worth every brave step. Feel it and let go of the calcification around your heart. And oh, pleaeeeeeeese go watch Brené Brown's TED Talk on vulnerability, if you haven't already. You won't regret it!

Imagination

With each imaginative idea released, your power comes alive,
Unlock your full potential, and watch your dreams strive and then thrive!

Imagination is a remarkable force that can transform the ordinary into the extraordinary, expanding your dreams and possibilities. As a child, I fully embraced the spirit of imagination, often speaking of my future as if it were already unfolding. My art teacher affectionately dubbed me 'Gunna' because of my habit of declaring what I would do next – a testament to my visionary outlook long before reality caught up. Ha. Well, that's what I like to tell myself anyway!

Though the link between imagination and emotional intelligence may not seem obvious, they are intertwined. Imagination enhances empathy, allowing you to understand the feelings of others, even when their experiences differ from your own. It also opens pathways to personal growth, enabling you to envision positivity, craft new narratives, and break free from rigid emotional patterns.

Ground yourself in the power of imagination. Look up ways to access the creative right side of the brain, such as changing your surroundings or drawing something with your opposite hand. A vibrant imagination equips you to move through life's challenges, transforming obstacles into opportunities for growth. When chaos threatens, let your imagination be your guide, helping you to rise above it and reshape your reality.

In essence, imagination is creative problem-solving: envisioning fresh ways of thinking. Say you wish to stop yelling at your partner because they're always late, go to a quiet space and visualise different ways you could respond and creative approaches to handling the situation.

Here's a magical page for your imagination to run wild and free.

Here are some reflections and ponderings to encourage you to think outside the box.

♥ How do you currently use your imagination to navigate life?
Reflect on moments where imagination has allowed you to envision new possibilities or make decisions creatively. Are there areas in your life where you could engage in it more?

♥   How do you handle moments when your imagination seems stifled or
dormant? The five senses may be a way in. When I am writing, I like to picture
myself in a conversation with my reader, visualising their face and expressions.
What practices or activities can you incorporate to reignite your creative spark
when you're feeling stuck?

♥   What dreams or desires have you envisioned but not yet acted upon?
What's stopping you from moving toward them? How might you break free
from limiting beliefs and use your imagination to craft a path forward?

♥　In what ways can you use your imagination to enhance your emotional intelligence? Consider how imagining different perspectives could help you better understand others' emotions, needs, and motivations.

♥　What would your 'best self' look like? If you were to imagine the most emotionally aware, resilient version of yourself, what traits would you possess? How can you start cultivating those qualities today?

• • •

As we close this entry, remember: your imagination is a powerful tool. Transform the ordinary into the extraordinary; think beyond boundaries; and embrace creativity! Your life is a masterpiece in the making – so keep dreaming, exploring, and reimagining all that it could become. Let your mind soar!

Charisma

Spark in every glance,
laughter dances through the room –
magnetism blooms.

Charisma is more than charm or social ease; it's the powerful blend of emotional intelligence and authenticity that creates a truly magnetic presence. It's what draws people in – not with pretence, but with a genuine openness that invites connection. When you put some effort into and nurture charisma, you transform not only how others respond to you but also the depth and beauty of your connections. It's a kind of magic: one that builds bridges and makes you unforgettable.

I was fortunate to witness this magic firsthand through my parents, both natural 'people's people'. Over the years, our family hosted numerous students from Japan. They would arrive in our home with limited language skills, and I would see them respond positively to Mum's nurturing and Dad's comedic ways: a couple of them came way out of their shells. My parents had a wonderful knack of making newcomers feel at ease in their company. It went beyond having a beautiful house, and serving delicious food: they celebrated every individual who walked through the door. They created an atmosphere of warmth and belonging, where everyone felt seen and valued.

At home, whether during lively gatherings or quiet moments shared over stories, I was surrounded by the energy that confidence, presence, and genuine enthusiasm bring. Watching them, I learnt that charisma isn't about impressing others; it's about igniting something real within them.

This upbringing shaped how I approach relationships: showing up fully, with vulnerability, curiosity, and a genuine desire to connect. Imagine what might shift in your life if you allowed yourself to embody that kind of presence. Imagine the connections, the possibilities, the impact. Because when you light up, you give others permission to do the same.

Now, I invite you to reflect on your own charisma. Ask yourself:

♥ *Is anything holding you back from fully embracing your charismatic self? Reflect on any fears, habits, or limiting beliefs that could be dimming your natural light, and consider how you might begin to shift the dial on those.*

♥ *What moments in your life have showcased your charismatic qualities? Think about times when you felt particularly engaged with or connected to others.*

♥ *How do you express warmth and enthusiasm in your interactions? Consider the ways you invite others into conversations or make them feel valued.*

♥ *What traits do you admire in charismatic individuals? Identify qualities you'd like to cultivate more in yourself.*

♥ *In what settings do you feel most confident and charismatic? Reflect on environments where you shine and identify how you can re-create that energy elsewhere.*

• • •

Charisma isn't some kind of gift you have to be born with to possess – it's a skill anyone can master. It's about connecting authentically, being fully present, and making others feel seen and valued. Step into your light, radiate warmth, and listen with intention. The more you embrace your true self, the more magnetic you'll become. Ready to own your charisma? The world is waiting for your luminescence! Enjoy the room, work your magic, be a spark!

Wounds of Childhood

The past may sting with shadows and pain,
But to the inner child, let love reign.
Beneath the stars and the soft twilight,
Your healing work will set things right.

In the midst of negativity or conflict, it's easy to internalise others' harsh energy and wonder if it's somehow your fault. But what if that feeling of self-blame runs deeper? What if it traces back to childhood wounds that were never fully acknowledged or healed?

We all carry baggage from our early years – those formative experiences where shame, guilt, or feeling 'not good enough' can take root. These patterns are tough to break, and while it's essential to protect yourself by setting boundaries and limiting time with toxic people, it's just as important to explore why you've taken on their negativity in the first place.

By understanding the roots of shame, you can start to separate your self-worth from others' actions. And that's where healing begins. Let's approach this with compassion, knowing that the journey toward self-acceptance is a process, especially when it comes from stuff that happened way back in our childhood. Some healing childhood ponderings ...

♥   *How did you feel as a child when you made a mistake or didn't meet expectations – was there a sense of shame or guilt that you still carry today?*

♥   *Can you remember any specific moments from your childhood where you felt 'not good enough' or unworthy of love and attention?*

♥   In what ways do you find yourself reacting to criticism or negativity today that might be rooted in unresolved childhood experiences?

♥   How do you separate your true self from the labels or judgements that others placed on you during your formative years?

♥   What would it look like for you to forgive that younger version of yourself who took on the hurt from others? How can you start showing compassion to that part of you now?

• • •

Remember, healing is a journey, and it begins with acknowledging your past and giving yourself permission to move forward. Be kind, patient, and compassionate with yourself – you're doing transformative work. Embrace your inner child, forgive those who couldn't give you what you needed, and honour the process of releasing old wounds. You are evolving, rewiring the patterns of the past, and breaking free from generational cycles. I'm so proud of you – of the little you, the teen you, and the incredible you who is standing here today!

There are countless gifted healers and space-holders ready to guide you through journeys into your past, help nurture your inner child, and support you in healing the wounds formed in your most vulnerable moments. Onward and upward!

Self-regulation

In the dance of emotions, find your flow,
Self-regulation whispers, 'Take it slow.'

Self-regulation is the beautiful art of aligning your emotions with your values, intentions, and the bigger picture of your life. In intense moments – falling in love, moving, or navigating loss – it's so easy to feel thrown off balance. But practising self-regulation gives you the power to pause, tune in, and respond intentionally instead of reacting impulsively. Mastering this skill helps you ride the waves of big emotions without getting swept away, navigate conflicts with grace, and stay steady even when life feels like it's on fast-forward. Acknowledge your emotions, honour them, and choose to express them with purpose – it's a game-changer for staying grounded and true to yourself.

Self-regulation tools? They're as unique as you are! For me, staying grounded means not sweating the small stuff, and letting go of what's out of my hands. To help me do that, I love to get wiggy with nature! I go full spiritual woo-woo, hugging trees, drawing mandalas in the sand, and channelling my inner child while frolicking in the ocean. I read clouds, sun-gaze, and soak in the elements like it's my job. Nature's where I feel my blessings, connecting to something bigger than myself. It shrinks my worries, reminding me how vast and wild life really is. (I was going to keep my tree-hugging ways secret, but *Married at First Sight* exposed me! Ha.)

Another way I stay balanced? Journalling – yep, just like this! But it doesn't stop there: take a peek at some other things I do to keep my energy steady and my life going smoothly. Keep an open heart, a curious mind, and a playful attitude as you explore these ideas. Who knows what might resonate with you. Life's always got its curveballs, but when you've self-regulation tools, you'll handle them like the powerhouse you are. You've got this, you grounded, fabulous, unstoppable force of nature!

Name your emotions.
Simply identifying what you're feeling and naming it can reduce the intensity and help you understand what's really going on. Get yourself an Emotions Wheel!

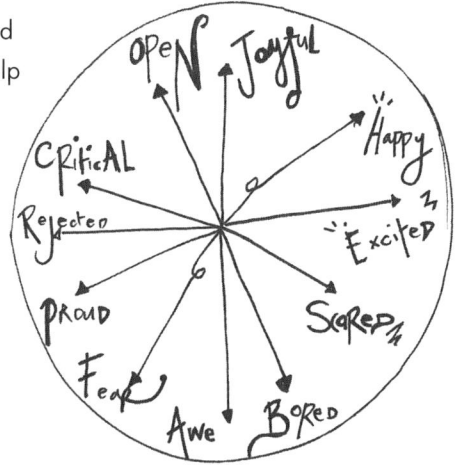

Pause and breathe. When emotions run high, take a moment to pause. Deep, slow breaths signal your nervous system to calm down, giving you space to think before reacting.

Avoid catastrophising. Stay grounded by challenging extreme thoughts. Ask yourself: is this as big as it feels right now? This helps you reframe and manage stress.

Take quiet time. Carve out space for yourself to recharge, whether through meditation, journalling, or simply unplugging from devices.

Stay curious. Ask yourself: why am I feeling this way? Self-awareness is key to self-regulation. Understanding triggers helps you to respond instead of react.

Set boundaries. Know your limits and communicate them clearly. Protecting your emotional energy prevents burnout and keeps you balanced.

Physical movement. Whether it's a walk, workout, or yoga, it helps release pent-up energy and stress. Bonus: it clears your mind too!

Build a supportive circle. Surround yourself with emotionally steady and self-aware people who inspire and encourage balance.

Get enough rest. Sleep impacts emotional regulation. Prioritise quality rest so you're less reactive and more resilient.

And some self-regulation questions to ponder ...

♥   What emotions do you find the hardest to regulate, and how might naming and understanding them change your response to challenging situations?

♥   What self-regulation tools or practices have you tried before, and which ones felt the most natural or effective for you?

♥   When was the last time you paused before reacting? How did it shift the outcome of that moment?

♥   What boundaries do you need to set – or strengthen – to protect your emotional energy and stay balanced?

♥   Think of someone in your life who seems emotionally steady. What qualities or habits do they have that inspire you, and how could you bring more of that energy into your own life?

• • •

When you experiment with these tools (and there are so many more!), as soon as you know something's not for you, drop it like it's hot! Invest your time in selecting and polishing the ones that work for you. You're like a diamond-hunter, looking for the most lustrous ways to feel balanced, empowered, and ready to handle anything. Can I get a whoop whoop?

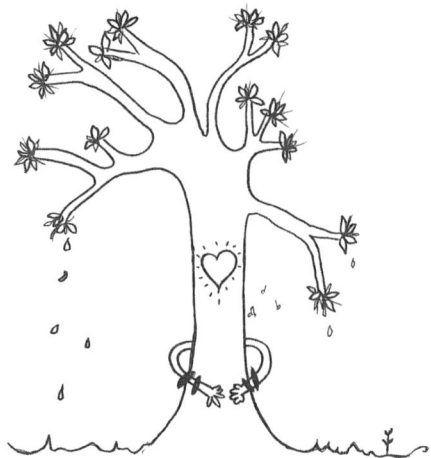

Gratitude

In this journal's embrace, let your heart unfold,
Pour out your gratitude, unfiltered and bold.

I wasn't always tuned in to the extraordinary power of gratitude to light the way. Resentment, bitterness, and discontent blocked me from feeling the flow of gratefulness in my life. I was busy focusing on what was lacking or what I perceived as wrong rather than what was present and positive. But through those tough times, when I dug deep enough, I learnt there was always something to be grateful for.

Science backs up the profound power of gratitude: it boosts dopamine and serotonin, lifting your mood and easing stress. Gratitude doesn't just elevate your mood, it changes your whole outlook. I lean into it daily, for warm hugs, sunny skies, or a yum meal. I keep an open dialogue with the Universe; often, I find myself whispering, 'Thank you, Universe, thank you', when overcome by life's beauty. Do you do that?

Take a moment today to pause and reflect on what you're thankful for.

♥ *What brought you joy today?*

♥ *Who made a positive impact on your life?*

♥ *Was there a simple pleasure that you overlooked today?*

SHINE YOUR LIGHT

♥ What challenge did you face today that helped you grow that you're grateful for?

♥ How did you make space for joy or creativity today?

A gratitude letter

I absolutely love writing letters – whether to my loved ones or to myself! I'd love you to write yourself a letter of gratitude, celebrating just how fabulous you are and all the amazing things you're doing in your life. Alternatively, write your name in the middle of the page, then surround it with words and phrases that reflect what you're thankful for about yourself. Let the gratitude flow!

• • •

Gratitude is everywhere. Sometimes it's about the tiniest thing! Be a gratitude detective, on the lookout for moments of joy. Start a gratitude journal, snap a daily pic of something or someone you're thankful for, or share with a loved one everything you love about them.

Now, my gratitude gush: I'm so thankful for *you*. The fact that you're holding this book and joining me on this journey is a true blessing. Thank you for your love, effort, and trust – it means the world! Ta, *gracias*, *terima kasih*, *obrigada*, *xiè xiè*, and dank u very much!

Dear ....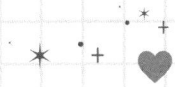

Me XXXXXX

Resilience

♔

From every shit storm that tests your might,
You rise anew, a beacon of light.

It's a bittersweet truth that lots of life's lessons are learnt the hard way – through our mistakes, challenges, and the mountains of hardship life sometimes heaps on us. It's undeniably tough – sometimes almost unbearable – but isn't it in those moments of adversity that you come face to face with your true strength? Those humbling experiences force you to pause, reflect, and take stock of where you are. Adversity is a relentless teacher, but when the road gets tough, remember: you're not just surviving – you're evolving. Every struggle carries the seed of transformation. With courage, you will rise stronger and brighter than before.

Resilience is one of the most essential qualities in this wild, messy, and beautiful life! There are times when I find myself thinking, *Help! I didn't sign up for this!* and wishing I would wake up and find it's all a bad dream. But then, somehow, it passes. By hanging in there, I turn that 'poo pile' into rich fertiliser, planting new seeds, and eventually harvesting greater resilience.

It's the challenges and lessons that life throws at you that build inner strength, empowering you to bounce back when things knock you off your path. Think of resilience as a muscle: each time you face adversity and navigate it, you come out stronger. For me, personal experiences like illness, heartbreak, and loss have shown me exactly what I'm made of.

Some resilience inquiry here:

♥ *Think of a recent challenge you faced. What emotions did you experience, and how did you respond? What did you learn from that situation?*

♥ *Consider a time when a setback led to personal growth. How did this experience reshape your perspective or approach to life?*

♥ List three strengths you possess that helped you move through tough times.

-

-

-

♥ What is a belief you've held about yourself or the world that was challenged by a difficult experience, and how did shifting or reaffirming that belief contribute to your resilience?

♥ *When was the last time you surprised yourself by overcoming something you thought was beyond your capacity? What inner resource or external support did you tap into that you didn't realise was available?*

• • •

You've got this, ya fabulously steadfast human! Every stumble and challenge you face only strengthens your resilience. Rising from those moments is where the real growth happens. Draw on your secret weapons, your creativity and adaptability – the art of bending without breaking, like a tree swaying in the wind yet standing tall. Resilience is also cultivated through tiny, deliberate steps – regulating your nervous system, finding grounding routines, or simply allowing yourself to rest. Life can be tough, no doubt, but what a wild ride it is. Honestly, I wouldn't trade these lessons in for anything! You're bringing the grit!

Hello gorgeous,

I hear you, and I'm so sorry that life's been throwing relentless chaos your way. It's tough when you're in the middle of the storm, isn't it? But here's the truth I've learnt: when life hurls its curveballs, the best thing you can do is try to ride things out with as much grace and surrender as possible. I know, easier said than done. But resisting what's out of our control only wears us down. Remember: this too shall pass, and even the hardest storms are part of a grander design meant to build resilience and deepen our wisdom.

I'll never forget when my world seemed to shatter all at once. I broke up with someone I loved, suffered a severe back injury, had a brutal fallout with a close friend, endured an invasive police search at a festival, got a speeding ticket, and fought an insurance battle over something that wasn't my fault. It felt like every day brought a new disaster. Each fresh challenge was another layer of my life crumbling beneath me, and no matter how much I begged the Universe for relief, more kept falling apart. It was stressful, outrageous, and deeply disheartening.

But eventually, I hit a point where I had to surrender, breathe, and return to gentleness. I had to let go of resisting the chaos and trust that the storm would eventually pass. That time shook me to my core, but it also taught me about my inner strength. I had to strip life back to basics and rebuild with care, and I came out stronger.

These storms, as exhausting as they are, won't last forever. They teach us profound lessons and show us what we're really made of. Take a step back when you can, try to see the bigger picture, and remember to seek the hidden gems in the madness. While it's easy to feel defeated when it pours and pours, these storms are often catalysts for growth, pushing us to leap forward in ways we might not even see at first.

The winds will eventually calm. Trust that you'll find peace on the other side – you've got this, gorgeous!

With so much love,
X Lu

• • •

Don't think for a minute I'm urging you to compromise who you are – show up authentically and flow with the beat of each moment. Know when to move, when to rest, and when to stand firm. Flexibility doesn't mean breaking – it means finding strength in softness and clarity in your choices.

RELATIONSHIPS

++*+*

Relationships are the heartbeats of your life — messy, magical, and meaningful. They shape who you are while reminding you who you're meant to be.

Whether you're an extrovert, an introvert, or somewhere in between (I'm an ambivert!), connection is vital. Humans, for the most part, are social creatures. How blessed are we to walk this life alongside the people we love? They might trigger us at times, but there's something profoundly beautiful about witnessing our loved ones — and being witnessed by them — through every stage and version of ourselves.

Stable relationships are critical to your sense of safety in the world. They are simultaneously challenging, spurs to growth, harbingers of pain (love and loss are two sides of the same coin), and, to me, the most precious gifts of our lifetime.

I love my family deeply, and I know how privileged I am to be able to say that. Not everyone can. That said, it hasn't always been easy — we've had our share of conflicts, challenges, and disagreements — but forgiveness and moving forward have always been our guiding principles. That's how Mum and Dad raised us, and it's given me a solid foundation to extend kindness and understanding beyond our family hearth and into the world.

The same holds true for my cherished friends, where I've also learnt to give and receive forgiveness along the way. I have friends who've been by my side since primary school; others from high school; and I have gained so many treasures from my tripping around the world. These friendships have aligned perfectly with the different ages and stages of my life and earthly incarnations.

When I was on *Married at First Sight*, I was told I could only invite ten guests to my wedding. My original list was 25. I cried when I had to narrow it down and begged to stretch it at least to 12 by assigning roles to two close friends (witchy-woo friend with chicken wing incoming! – when you know, you know). Even so, the fact that some of my dearest people couldn't be there felt like a loss. It reminded me how much I value my connections and how relationships are the threads that bind our lives together.

Intimate relationships have always been a deep passion of mine. Through the seven serious partnerships I've experienced, I've gained incredible insight, adventure, and love. Each partner entered my life at just the right time, bringing lessons and moments that shaped me in ways I'll forever cherish. Now, as I look to the future, I hold a quiet hope of finding my everlasting love – one built on mutual respect, trust, and a shared vision for the journey ahead.

Over time, I've come to see relationships as remarkable mirrors, reflecting not only our strengths but also our shadows. It's a vulnerable and transformative space, requiring honesty and courage to stand fully seen by another.

Life has taught me to move beyond the trap of co-dependency and instead embrace relationships rooted in interdependence – a beautiful dance that honours individuality while weaving together a shared life. These are the partnerships that allow room for growth, celebrate each other's separate worlds, and bring all the heart, depth, and richness of true connection. Here's to the adventure of love, in all its forms!

• • •

Humans are endlessly fascinating, aren't we? Walking down the street, I often find myself wondering about the lives of others: *What's their story? Are they okay? What's their relationship like with their family?* To me, even the briefest interactions with strangers – the fleeting 'freckling' of relationships – can hold a unique beauty.

Through years of being open to opportunities to connect, including working in hospitality, tour leading, being a practitioner/healer, and creating spaces like 'Soulful Speed Dating', I've learned so much about the art of relating. Whether it's been serving cocktails in tropical resorts or holding space at workshops and tantra festivals, these experiences taught me how people show up, listen, and navigate the dynamics of connection. There are infinite ways to relate, and we're all just figuring it out as we go.

• • •

This section dives into the many layers of relationships: family bonds, lifelong friendships, intimate partnerships, and, most importantly, the relationship you have with yourself. That one never stops evolving, does it? I hope this section of the book gives you plenty to reflect on, guiding you through the nitty gritty and leaving you with new tools and clarity about how you relate to the world around you.

My hope is that you will be inspired to pause and consider the relationships in your life: the ones that uplift you and help shape who you are. Who are the people you have fun with or solve the world's problems with? Who brings you healing chicken soup? Who's patient enough to really tease out what you are thinking and feeling? Who sees you? Time is precious, and the connections we nurture define so much of our experience and outlook. Don't forget to tell your peeps how much you love them!

• • •

I'm endlessly grateful for my special humans – both my family and my chosen soul family. They see me, love me, and accept me in all of my light and shadow. And I'm grateful for you, too, for being here and going to all these places with me. We're growing our emotional intelligence so much! Bring it on!

Relationships Inventory

Who's lifting you up, who's helping you grow?
Time to check the vibes and let the good ones know ...

... that they are precious! Now that you've taken a deep dive into the building blocks of *knowing thyself* and have laid a strong foundation for how the branches of emotional intelligence sway and groove together, it's time to turn the spotlight outward. Let's roll out your *relationship inventory* and reflect on who's in your life so you can count your blessings! And here's a fun twist – who might be missing?

Think of this as a playful and heartfelt scribble-it-out relationship quiz to explore the rich tapestry of relationships that shape your world. This will be fun!

♥   *Who in your life feels like your rock? That person who's always there for you when the chips are down. How do you show them your gratitude?*

♥   *Who is your best friend? Maybe it's a human or a furry companion – or maybe you're lucky to have many. What makes them so special to you?*

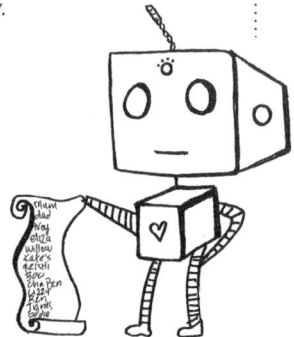

♥ Who makes you laugh until your belly aches? Celebrate the gift of joy they bring into your life. What makes them so funny?

♥ Is there a family member you no longer speak to but wish you did? If you feel ready, what would it take to rekindle that connection? And if it's not the right time, what small steps might you take to find peace with the situation?

♥ *Who do you miss who has left this earthly plane? How do you honour their memory or keep their essence alive in your life? What symbols or rituals (could even be opening a photo album) help you feel their love close by?*

♥ *What three words describe your relationship with your family? Let it be an honest snapshot – celebrate the good; acknowledge the hard.*

♥ *When was the last time you shared a playful moment with a stranger –*
like a smile, a compliment, or even a little flirtation? How did it light you
and them up?

♥ *Is there someone you think of as 'the one that got away'? What lessons*
did they bring into your life, and how have they helped you evolve?

♥ *Who in your life feels difficult or toxic at times? What boundaries or shifts could help you feel freer and more balanced in that relationship*

♥ *Is there a type of person you'd love to welcome into your life? Someone adventurous, wise, or funny? How can you create space to beckon them in?*

Extra with your texta

♥ *What have you learnt?*

♥ *Have you surprised yourself with any of your answers?*

♥ *If you were to repeat this exercise in six months, which questions would you hope to answer differently?*

• • •

Well done, you! I challenged you with some really random contemplations there. I love a bit of the unexpected! Every relationship, from the closest bonds to passing moments with strangers, is a chance to connect, learn, and grow. Be kind to yourself as you explore these questions, and remember: the most important relationship is always the one you have with yourself. Boooyah, let's go!

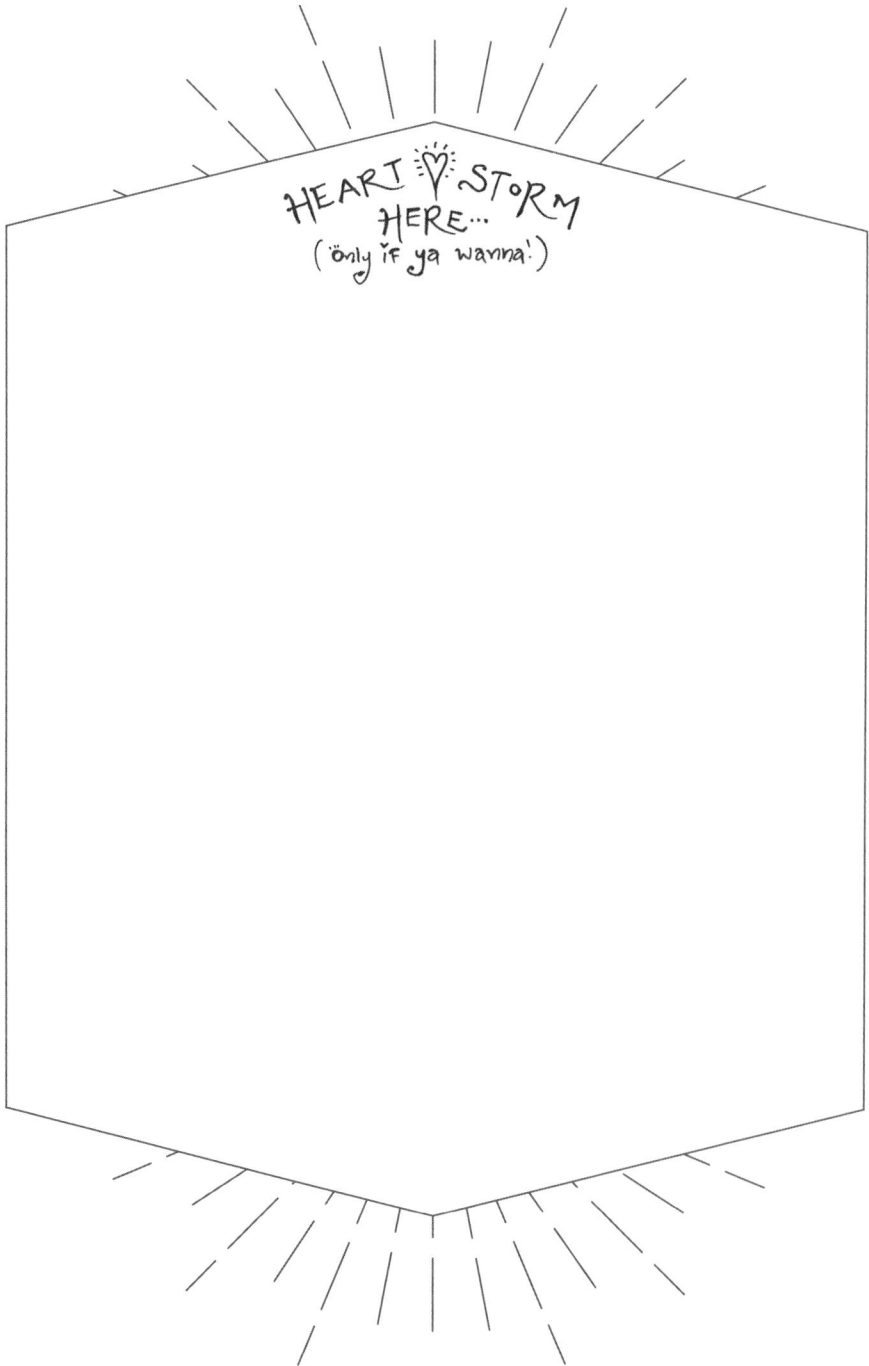

HEART ♡ STORM
HERE...
(only if ya wanna!)

Social Skills

😀

Speak with purpose, listen well,
In every exchange, let kindness swell.
Social grace is more than talk,
It's in the way we walk the walk.

Social skills are the unsung heroes of a fulfilling life. No matter where you fall on the spectrum of social ease – from life-of-the-party extrovert to quiet observer – there's always room to grow. The good news? Social skills aren't fixed: they're learnt, refined, and enriched with practice and guidance. With a little awareness and effort, you can become a master of the art: knowing how to connect, communicate, stand your sacred ground, and honour the unique contributions of everyone around you.

Let's be real – effective communication, conflict resolution, teamwork, and relationship-building are the bedrock of strong, meaningful connections. My hope is that this journey helps you feel confident in your social abilities while surrounding yourself with people who celebrate you just as you are. Let's explore the art of connection together!

Now then – here's some tips to elevate your social skills! If you're already the master of this domain, move on ahead to another entry that's calling you.

Active listening is key.
Truly hear what others are saying. Nod (not excessively), maintain eye contact, and show engagement with verbal cues like 'I see' or 'That's interesting'. Avoid thinking about your response while they're still talking – be fully present.

Master the art of small talk.
Small talk may seem trivial, but it's a gateway to building trust and rapport. I love doing it at 'meet and greets' during my shows. It's a gorgeous moment of connection. Ask light-hearted questions like, 'How's your day going?'

Read the room.

Pay attention to the energy in the room. Are people feeling playful or serious? Adjust your tone and contributions to match the vibe while staying authentic. If you're really masterful – you can elevate it with your on-point high vibes!

Practise empathy.

Put yourself in someone else's shoes. Try to understand their emotions and perspectives before responding. A little empathy goes a long way in creating deeper connections.

Know when to take space.

Standing your sacred ground doesn't mean dominating conversations. It's about knowing when to step back, when to speak up, and when to let others shine.

Learn to say no kindly.

Boundaries are part of healthy communication. When you can't do something, say it with kindness: 'I'd love to help, but I don't have the bandwidth right now.'

Adapt to different communication styles.

Not everyone expresses themselves the same way. Some are direct; others prefer subtlety. Stay flexible and be willing to meet people where they're at.

Share a bit of yourself.

Vulnerability builds trust. Share something personal (but appropriate) to deepen connections: 'That reminds me of a time when ...' or 'I can relate to that because ...'

Focus on collaboration, not competition.

Whether it's teamwork or friendship, look for ways to uplift and support rather than compete. When others feel valued, relationships thrive.

Use humour wisely.

A good laugh can break the ice, but keep your humour inclusive and kind. Avoid jokes that could alienate or offend others.

Pause before you react.

When emotions run high, take a moment to breathe before responding. Thoughtful reactions lead to better outcomes and fewer misunderstandings.

Practise gratitude and appreciation.

A simple 'thank you' or acknowledgement of someone's effort strengthens relationships. Gratitude leaves a lasting positive impression.

Be curious, not judgemental.

Instead of jumping to conclusions about someone's actions or opinions, ask questions to understand their perspective. This fosters trust and openness.

Don't fear awkwardness.

Conversations don't always flow perfectly, and that's okay. A little humour or a genuine acknowledgment like, 'I'm not sure what to say next!' can lighten the moment. I've learnt to love a bit of 'awks and dorks' these days!

Surround yourself with growth-oriented people.

Spend time with those who inspire you to communicate better, listen deeply, and build stronger connections. Social skills are contagious!

Celebrate your wins.

Whether you navigated a tough conversation or sparked a meaningful connection, take a moment to acknowledge your progress. Growth happens in small steps.

• • •

Incorporating these tips into your daily life will help you build confidence in social situations and create deeper, more meaningful connections with others. It might seem like a lot at first, so start small: try practising one or two at a time. Even printing them out and reading through them occasionally will help rewire your subconscious, making you more naturally equipped in future interactions. Remember, social skills are a superpower – strengthen them, and watch your relationships thrive!

Consider the following reflective questions:

♥   *How do you show up in conversations? Are you actively listening, engaging, or are you distracted and waiting for your turn to speak?*

♥   *What's your go-to response in moments of conflict? Do you react defensively, shut down, or try to resolve it with empathy and understanding?*

♥   *How do you adapt to different personalities or communication styles? Are you flexible in your approach, or do you stick rigidly to your own way of interacting?*

♥   *What feedback have you received over the years about how you communicate? Have friends, colleagues, or family pointed out areas where you shine or could improve?*

♥   *How comfortable are you with vulnerability and authenticity? Do you communicate openly and honestly, or do you hold back out of fear of judgement? What's something truly authentic and vulnerable about your social skills that you could write down right now? Are there any 'Achilles' heels' you can pinpoint and express with honesty?*

• • •

Shiny social skills? They're your ticket to unforgettable moments and authentic connections. Every chat is a chance to lift someone up and spread some magic. Let your vibe be bright – because the best part of humanity is the way you connect and make people feel! People are often quick to forget what you say but remember the way that you made them feel. Go out and light up the world!

Generosity and Emotional Impact

Generosity isn't just about giving – it's about unlocking abundance for everyone, including yourself. The magic? The more you pour out, the more your heart overflows and grows.

I hold generosity as one of my highest values, not just in a material sense, but in generosity of heart and spirit. To me, true generosity is about entering every space with the intention of elevating it, leaving people feeling better than when I found them, and creating a positive ripple effect. It's a wonderful way to express emotional intelligence.

When I engage with others, I want people to feel seen, valued, and special. That might be through a thoughtful gift, a kind word, a meaningful touch (with consent, of course) or simply being fully present by offering my undivided attention. Being generous in terms of making people feel important and understood isn't just about grand gestures; it's about bringing whatever you have to every situation and asking yourself, 'How can I use my resources, my energy, my presence to create something magical and beneficial for everyone in this moment? How can I make it better?' But whether it's money, time, or attention, giving freely inspires growth, not just in others, but within ourselves as well.

Here are some prompts to get you energised around being a more generous person:

♥ *How can you give back, either to a stranger or a loved one?*
Be unexpected. Come up with something that's more generous than your usual.
Make that commitment now. What is it?

♥ *I'd love you to do a cheeky 'generosity audit' of your last week, not just*
estimating what you did with money, but also with your time, attention, and
energy. Where in your life have you been generous?

♥   *Write down areas in your life where you could be more generous,*
whether in your relationships, at work, or within your community.

Here are some generosity tips to get your juices flowing ...

- Spend quality time with a loved one, dedicate time to listen to a friend in need. Make a conscious effort to give them your full attention – no distractions, no interruptions.

- Be generous with your compliments. Offer words of encouragement. Do it often; it costs nothing.

- Plan a series of small, thoughtful acts, like surprising a friend with a gift, volunteering, or cooking a meal for someone going through a tough time.

- Each morning, take five minutes to visualise yourself giving in different ways throughout the day, whether through a smile, a kind gesture, or an unexpected gift.

- Find ways to give without the recipient knowing it was you, whether it's through a charitable donation, leaving a small gift for someone, or paying for a stranger's meal.

Emotional Impact

The embodiment of emotional intelligence is choosing to show up in a generous way – even when life isn't serving you its best. When you are fully present, authentic, and have good intention and energy, you don't just make your own world better, you become inspiring for others. Before walking in the door of a party or gathering, I always make a point of checking in with myself. I consciously push aside anything that might pull the energy down.

Imagine yourself as a pebble dropped into a calm pond. The ripples are your energy and emotions, and they spread far and wide, touching everything and everyone around you. Every day, whether you're conscious of it or not, you're creating waves that shape the mood and vibe of those in your orbit. That's emotional contagion – your invisible yet undeniable superpower.

The question is: what kind of ripples do you want to send out? Joy and empathy? Or stress and negativity? You are way more powerful than you give yourself credit for.

♥   *Reflect on a time when you walked into a room and immediately felt positive energy. How did the atmosphere lift your mood?*

♥   *Recall an instance when your mood positively or negatively influenced those around you. What did that look like, and what did you learn from that experience?*

♥ Pay attention to the emotional states of people you interact with over the next few days. How do their emotions influence your feelings and actions?

♥ Can you become more aware of the emotional states you inject into spaces?

♥ Choose one person in your life to focus on this week. How can you intentionally send out ripples of positivity to them?

• • •

Being generous boosts your 'helper's high', releasing feel-good chemicals like dopamine and oxytocin. Generosity reduces stress, increases happiness, and even improves health – generous people tend to have lower blood pressure and live longer, more fulfilled lives. So, every act of kindness both benefits others and enhances your own wellbeing. Make it happen, you divine thing!

Get cReaTive HeRe...

Boundaries

Boundaries aren't walls; they're bridges to mutual respect. Protecting your peace while honouring theirs, teaching the art of connection without compromise.

Boundaries are necessary for emotional wellbeing, personal growth, and healthy relationships. While learning to communicate them can feel uncomfortable initially, it's an empowering practice that creates deeper connections. I wasn't raised with the language of boundaries and had to learn to identify, set, and communicate them over time, after discovering the concept about a decade ago. Setting boundaries creates safety because those around you understand where they stand. However, not everyone will feel comfortable with you setting boundaries. Some will find it confronting or inconvenient. How do you feel about expressing boundaries?

I deeply value people who can express their boundaries with clarity, kindness, and a healthy balance of firmness and flexibility. Some folks are still learning the ropes, and their attempts can come off a little rigid – like a stern school principal. The secret ingredient is tone; it can make all the difference when it comes to delivering a boundary with kindness. Normalising conversations about boundaries is essential for developing emotional intelligence and fostering healthy relationships. So, here's to celebrating boundaries!

Here are some of my non-negotiables:

- I will not tolerate any form of emotional or physical abuse.

- I need space and alone time to recharge and create, even in intimate relationships.

- I value open and honest communication in all close relationships.

Finding and setting your boundaries

Boundaries evolve with time – they're not static. Sometimes they need strengthening for safety, and other times, they can be relaxed for growth. Reflecting on your emotions and needs intermittently can help you clarify where you need to set your own personal boundaries.

♥   *What are your boundaries?*

♥ *What situations make you feel uncomfortable or resentful? What triggers those feelings?*

♥ *How does your body react when a boundary is crossed? Do you feel tension, fatigue, or stress?*

♥ *When was the last time you felt overwhelmed? Could setting stronger boundaries have helped?*

♥ *Is there someone who tends to cross your boundaries? If so, how can you communicate with them clearly and kindly that their behaviour is not acceptable, in order to protect yourself more effectively?*

♥ *How comfortable are you in setting and communicating your boundaries to others?*

Once you have established where you need boundaries in your life, you need to set and express them to those around you. If you're new to boundaries, start small. Practise saying 'no' kindly, using statements like, 'I can't commit to that right now', and use 'I' statements to express needs without blame, such as, 'I need quiet time after work to recharge.'

• • •

I'm proud of you! Setting boundaries isn't just a practice, it's an act of self-love and respect that strengthens your emotional resilience and the genuine connections you form with others, keeping you and them safe. While it may feel daunting at first, the more you embrace and communicate your limits with compassion, the more you create the space for genuine, fulfilling relationships to thrive.

Pause...
Feel youR
HEART &
bReathe...
☆ 1234
inHale → Hold...
1234, Exhale
RepeaT ♡

Good Communication

Speak with kindness, hear with care,
Words can heal and show you're there.
A little patience, a lot of grace,
Good communication lights the space!

I received a masterclass in effective communication during my time living in Byron Bay, particularly while residing with individuals committed to conscious communication. We embraced the practice of voicing what didn't feel right, creating a safe and supportive environment for open dialogue, even when it was hard. This experience taught me the profound impact of honest conversations on relationships and personal growth.

Effective communication is the cornerstone of any healthy relationship. It shapes our connections, influences our interactions, and significantly impacts how we understand and relate to one another. In a world filled with noise, the ability to communicate clearly, kindly, and honestly is a gift that can foster deeper understanding and stronger bonds.

Being an excellent communicator is not just about being articulate; it's about creating a safe space for open dialogue. It involves listening deeply, acknowledging others' feelings, and expressing our own needs and desires without fear. When we communicate effectively, we invite vulnerability, allowing us to engage authentically and foster a sense of belonging.

To deepen your awareness of your communication style and those around you, consider observing how you and others engage in conversations. Understanding diverse communication styles can significantly strengthen relationships.

Communication tips

Be authentic.
There's nothing more awesome than being authentic in your communication style and feeling the freedom to express yourself honestly and from the heart.

Know your audience.
Tailor your communication style to suit people's needs and preferences. Consider their background and knowledge.

Be clear and concise.
Use simple and straightforward language to convey your message. Avoid jargon or overly complex terms that may be confusing.

Express yourself uniquely.
Master the art of being engaging and authentic. Keep some intriguing questions and witty (and perfectly appropriate) quotes ready to spark a great connection!

Active listening
As mentioned earlier in this journal, active listening is essential for healthy relationships. It requires two people to engage in respectful listening and open, thoughtful communication. In the past, I tended to get over-excited in conversations, eager to offer my opinions without always considering others as much as I do now. I could be a bit of a 'conversation bandit', rushing in opinions with unsolicited advice (face plant). Over time, life taught me the power of pausing and truly tuning in. Once I embraced active listening, my relationships deepened and became more fulfilling, with trust flourishing in the space between words.

   Active listening is more than hearing words: it's about fully engaging with someone, giving them your undivided attention, and being genuinely curious about their perspective. It requires us to hold our responses and absorb what the other person is sharing.

Here are some key aspects of active listening – and some simple exercises that can help transform your approach:

PARAPHRASING PRACTICE

This powerful tool involves restating what someone has said in your own words, showing genuine attention and allowing them to clarify their thoughts. Saying, 'So, what I'm hearing is ...' can greatly enhance your conversations.

> **Exercise:** Pair up and have one person share a story for two to three minutes while the other listens. The listener then paraphrases the message, and the speaker provides feedback to refine understanding.

OPEN-ENDED QUESTIONS DRILL

Instead of asking yes-or-no questions, use open-ended ones to invite deeper sharing and keep the dialogue flowing.

> **Exercise:** Create a list of topics, then formulate three open-ended questions for each. Engage with a partner using questions such as, 'How did that make you feel?', 'Can you expand on that?'

AVOIDING INTERRUPTIONS CHALLENGE

Interrupting can shut down conversations, so practising patience is vital.

> **Exercise:** Set a timer for five minutes. One person speaks while the other listens without interruptions. Afterward, the listener summarises the discussion and reflects on the experience.

TELL ME MORE TECHNIQUE

Encourage deeper sharing with phrases like, 'Tell me more about that' or 'Can you elaborate on that?'

> **Exercise:** Use this technique in conversations with a partner, then switch roles to experience both sides.

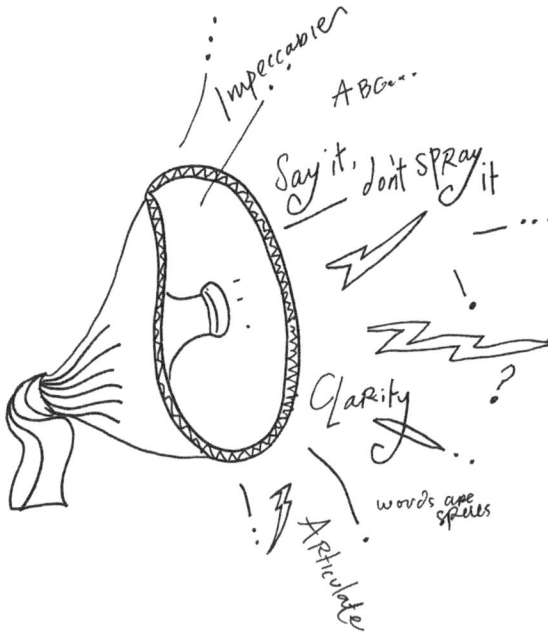

• • •

Active listening transforms social interactions and communication. Mastering it requires time, patience, and humility. By truly listening and engaging, you give others the invaluable gift of your full attention, demonstrating to them that what they say matters – they matter to you. When you listen, bring your whole self. Your full presence is the best gift you can give another.

Nonverbal communication and social observation

Enhance your nonverbal communication.
Be mindful of your body language, facial expressions, and tone of voice. Use open gestures and a warm tone to express approachability and connection.

♥   *How does your body language shift when you're confident compared to when you're anxious or defensive?*

♥   *Are there specific gestures or expressions you use that foster connection, or ones that may unintentionally create distance?*

Observe social cues.
Tune into others' body language, facial expressions, and tone of voice to gain a deeper understanding of their feelings and intentions.

♥   *How well do you read the room? What can you do to become more attuned to the unspoken signals of others?*

• • •

And ... watch out for unsolicited advice – both giving *and* receiving! Here's the truth bomb: sometimes, just mirroring and paraphrasing is way more powerful than dropping pearls of wisdom. Instead of playing guru, try asking epic questions that help someone figure it out themselves, or check if they're open to advice. I'm still working on this myself (ha! as I write a book on emotional intelligence, packed with advice – oh, the irony)! Let's keep tuning in together: you're a dazzling work in progress, just like me, and we're absolutely nailing it!

Jot down your good, bad, and gloriously messy thoughts right here!

Conflict

Conflict stirs like a storm in the night,
Shadows clash in the absence of light.
But through the struggle, a truth will evolve,
Peace finds its way; the heart will resolve.

Some of you might be absolute pros at managing conflict – and if that's you, feel free to skip ahead to another entry. For me, though, conflict resolution hasn't always come naturally. For much of my life, when backed into a corner, I'd react defensively – blaming, shaming, and seeing the other person as my opponent. Not exactly my finest moments.

Thankfully, life – and the incredible people I've encountered and journeyed with along the way – has been a patient teacher. I've learnt to communicate with clarity, approach situations with more empathy, and see disagreements not as battles to win, but as opportunities for connection and understanding. It's a skill I'm deeply grateful for – and one I'm committed to refining with every conflict that presents itself.

Another transformative experience for me was studying and completing a course in Nonviolent Communication (NVC) and diving into books on the topic. This approach is so simple yet profoundly effective – it truly revolutionised the way I view and handle conflict. It also shed light on just how reactive and, at times, harsh my previous conflict management style had been.

In my younger years, I'd quickly resort to blame or raising my voice over something trivial, like not getting a turn with the TV remote. Now I approach conflict by seeking to understand the other person's perspective and checking in with my own feelings. I calmly state the issue, share how it affects me – without blame – and negotiate a solution that works for everyone. Since practising NVC, everything has shifted positively. And, funnily enough, I don't even own a TV anymore!

Navigating conflict from a place of kindness and compassion – rather than defensiveness or aggression – creates an environment where connection thrives and resolution becomes possible. It's not about avoiding conflict but facing it with tools that foster understanding, respect, and care for everyone involved. This work, while challenging at times, is some of the most rewarding I've ever done.

Some conflict-resolution strategies

Stay calm.
Try to remain calm and composed during conflicts. Take deep breaths and focus on finding a solution rather than escalating the situation. You might just need some time out to re-regulate and come back to it when you're feeling centred.

Express yourself clearly.
Use 'I' statements to express your thoughts and feelings without blaming or accusing the other person. Be specific about the issue and what you would like to see change.

Seek understanding.
Try to understand the other person's point of view and the underlying reasons for their feelings or actions. This can help you find common ground and work toward a resolution.

Focus on solutions.
Instead of dwelling on the problem, focus on finding a solution that meets the needs of both parties. Brainstorm possible solutions together and be open to compromise.

Take responsibility.
Be willing to take responsibility for your part in the conflict and apologise if it feels genuine (check out the four-step apology online). This can help defuse tensions and create a more positive atmosphere for resolution.

Think of someone you have had conflict with in the past or can be in regular arguments with now. Get honest with yourself and ask:

♥   *What emotions do you feel when conflict arises, and how does that influence your response?*

♥   How can you express your needs and concerns in a way that promotes understanding and resolution?

♥   What patterns from past conflicts are you noticing in this situation, and what can you learn from them? Are they familiar?

♥   What are you willing to do to create a solution, and how can you stay open to kind resolve?

• • •

Conflict doesn't have to be the enemy – it can be a bridge to deeper understanding and connection. Every disagreement is an opportunity to refine your emotional tools and grow stronger in your relationships. By approaching conflict with intention, compassion, and the right mindset, you can transform challenges into lasting, meaningful resolutions. Tackle with kindness!

Triggers and Projection

Between the trigger and your reply,
Insert a pause where choices lie.
In that pause, calm and clear,
You'll grow and find freedom here.

In shadows cast, can you see your own fears?
Projecting on others, you mask what appears.
Look closely within, let truth break the mould,
For what's in your heart is a story untold.

While they are very different, being triggered – having stormy emotional reactions – and projecting – attributing your feelings to external sources – are patterns of behaviour that have their roots in childhood. Both can hinder the development of good emotional intelligence.

Triggers

Triggers are like emotional landmines – unexpected, explosive, and often out of proportion to the situation. They're usually tied to old wounds you didn't even realise were still raw. What makes them tricky is that you can't predict when or where they'll go off, and when they do, they can stir up chaos – sometimes for everyone in the vicinity. Whether it's a stranger rattling your nerves or a family conflict where a single comment sends you spiralling into frustration or hurt, it can get messy (bless this mess!).

Here's a personal confession: I've had my own battles with triggers, especially when interacting with family. I've worked very hard on that old part of me that used to lash out with passive aggression, say something mean or just be, you know, sarcastic! It was as if my deep emotions would hijack my amygdala, leaving me operating on pure instinct – like I had to aggressively push the person away to protect myself – rather than be reasonable or understanding.

Taming that fiery part of me has been one of the most transformative journeys of my life. And, I've gotta say, it hasn't been easy. Lots of accountability. There's been so much ego to unpack, so many moments where I've had to confront the uncomfortable truth about how I show up in situations of conflict or vulnerability.

These days, when a trigger flares up (and yes, they still do), I've learnt to pause and feel it fully. Because here's the thing: *you have to feel to heal.* I slow down, take deep breaths, and ask myself what's really going on. Is this about the moment at hand, or is it connected to something deeper – an old wound, an unmet need, or a story I've been carrying for too long?

Then, I connect with my highest self – the grounded, thoughtful part of me that responds with kindness and clarity, not sarcasm or passive aggression. It's a conscious decision to let my reactions come from a place of calm presence, seeking solutions that benefit everyone, rather than a knee-jerk reaction that divides and wounds.

And here's the reward: every time I choose to respond thoughtfully instead of reacting impulsively, I feel stronger, lighter, and more loving. With practice, that behaviour gradually becomes habitual. Taming my triggers hasn't just improved my relationships, it's deepened my self-respect and my connection to who I truly am. Triggers aren't easy to face, but they are powerful opportunities for growth.

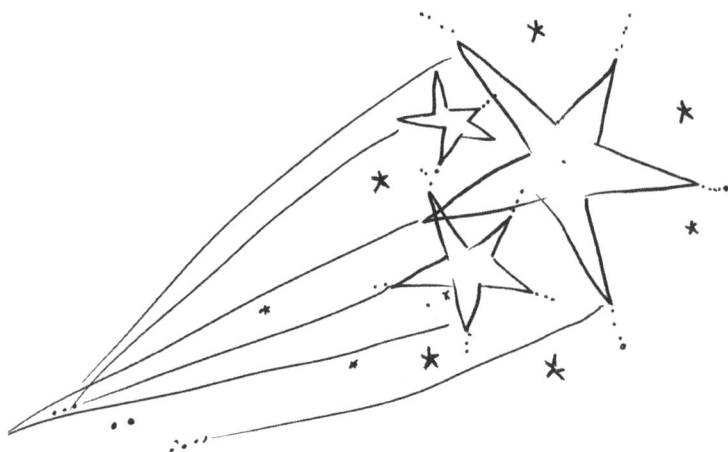

UNPACKING YOUR TRIGGERS

As you reflect, you may notice patterns in what triggers you. For example, if overconfident people annoy you, it might reveal insecurities about your self-esteem. Frustration with carefree individuals could indicate your own discomfort with letting go and being more 'out there' yourself. Recognising these triggers isn't about self-blame; it's about acknowledging parts of your emotional self that need attention. Ready to explore your triggers?

♥ *Can you recall a recent moment where you felt particularly triggered? What was it about the situation that led to such a strong reaction?*

♥ *What values or beliefs of yours are being challenged when you feel triggered?*

♥ *Does this experience remind you of a past moment when you felt similarly?*

♥ *What strategies can you use to soothe this emotion in the present, without overreacting?*

♥ *How can you turn this trigger into an opportunity for personal growth or learning?*

• • •

Triggers may keep showing up like uninvited guests at your party, but here's the deal: you can control how you respond to them. Yes, they're terrifying at times, but instead of running for the hills, think of it as a moment to enrol in 'Trigger Training'. Eventually, when they try to gatecrash your gathering, you'll be able to send them on their way and get straight back on the dancefloor. Cha-cha-cha.

Projection

Have you ever found yourself judging someone harshly, only to realise later that what you were so upset about actually reflected something in you? I know I have. There have been times in my life when I projected my own fears or unresolved issues onto an intimate partner. I would find myself reacting to them in ways that didn't make sense, or even accusing them of things they hadn't done, only to realise I was projecting my own insecurities, past relationship failures, and unhealed wounds onto them. It's tough to admit, but those moments have been some of the most humbling and enlightening in my journey toward healing.

One of the hardest lessons I've learnt is that our projections aren't just about the other person – they're a mirror showing us parts of ourselves we've avoided, suppressed, or haven't fully understood. It's a painful but powerful process, and it takes a lot of self-awareness and compassion to break free from it. But once you recognise it, there's freedom in it. You begin to see your own patterns and give yourself the chance to rewrite the story – without dragging the weight of the past into the present. This practice of noticing when you're projecting can help you rebuild relationships with more clarity and, ultimately, more love.

Understanding projections is key to bringing more awareness to them when they arise. After all, we're all works in progress, navigating life and supporting each other along the way. If you find yourself on the receiving end of a projection, resist the urge to shout, 'PROJECTION!' (as tempting as it might be!). Instead, take a moment to reflect.

Here are some powerful inquiries to help you unpack what's happening and get to the heart of the matter. Like every part of this book, some inquiries will be yours to answer and some might not be relevant. Take what's yours and leave the rest. You're doing great work!

♥   *Think of someone that really gets under your grill. What emotions or judgements do you feel toward this person? Can you trace the irritation back to a past experience or an unresolved feeling within yourself?*

♥   Keeping this same person in your thoughts – are you projecting an old fear or past hurt onto this situation or do you just generally find their essence annoying. Why? What is it about them?

♥   Is there a part of you that feels unseen or misunderstood in this situation, and how can you own that feeling without blaming others?

♥   Ready to dive deep? What does your reaction uncover about an unmet need or unresolved emotion within you? Is there a part of yourself you might be avoiding, rejecting, or finding difficult to embrace?

♥   How can you respond with compassion, both toward yourself and the person involved – whether you're projecting onto them or they're projecting onto you? How can you show up grounded and open, resisting the pull of judgement or defensiveness?

• • •

Next time you feel triggered and are spitting out projection, ask yourself: 'What is this moment trying to teach me about me?' That awareness is a game-changer. Embrace your projections as the quirky little signposts they are – pointing you toward growth, self-awareness, and a whole lot more freedom. Check your lens! Projection be gone!

Acceptance

★

The paradox, both curious and wise:
When you accept yourself and others, change will arise.

Radical acceptance has completely transformed how I view relationships and life. I'm not saying I now run around tolerating everything, but I recognise that everyone has their own unique story, shaped by their experiences and beliefs. Some people I interact with might have the emotional capacity of a plastic spoon (oops, Lu, a little judgy-wudgy there!), but it's not my job to change them: it's my job to meet them where they're at, whether our interaction is fleeting or something more lasting. Let go of the expectation that everyone should be a soup ladle!

When I find myself frustrated by someone's behaviour, I remind myself that we're all a product of how we were parented and the social conditioning we've absorbed along the way. Some folk never learnt how to express feelings without sounding like a robot, and others may think vulnerability is a foreign language. These days, I'm more inclined to pause, breathe, and remember that not everyone's emotional software aligns with mine, and that's okay.

Surprisingly, I find relief in accepting people exactly as they are. And I definitely do not compromise my values; it just means I create space for others to be their authentic selves while staying true to who I am. True inclusion means welcoming everyone without judgement, appreciating what they bring to the table – even if it's not what I anticipated. While it's important to be discerning about who you invite into your inner circle, remind yourself to approach each new person with curiosity: What can you learn from their perspective? What unique beauty can you discover and celebrate in them?

Letting go of the need to change or offer unsolicited advice is incredibly liberating and a great skill to practise. Let people express their true selves and celebrate them exactly where they're at, finding freedom in acceptance for both yourself and those around you. Here's a couple of things to ponder on with your 'acceptance' practice:

♥   Think of someone you find hard to accept. Instead of focusing on what's missing, try to appreciate what they are contributing, even if it's different from what you expect. What do you appreciate about them?

♥   Practise letting go of judgement and instead meet people with curiosity. What can you learn from this person's perspective?

♥   Think of a recent situation where you felt frustrated by someone's behaviour. What might their actions reflect about their experiences or struggles? How can you approach it with empathy rather than judgement?

♥   In what ways do you feel you impose your expectations on others? How could accepting someone's differences bring more peace to your interactions?

♥   How might your relationships transform if you focused on accepting people exactly as they are, rather than hoping they'd become who you want them to be? What would that shift in perspective allow you to experience?

• • •

Radical acceptance has helped me build deeper, more authentic connections with every kind of human spoon out there – be it a plastic one, a spork, or a soup ladle. It's best that I let go of the expectation that everyone should be a fancy soup ladle. And yes, that includes myself. I accept me – as flawed as I am fabulous! By honouring the individuality of others, I've learnt to approach relationships with more compassion and a whole lot less resistance. Huzzah!

Forgiveness

Forgiveness freckles the heart with sun:
Let resentment come undone!
Don't harbour the hate anchor for too long,
'Cause we're all human and we all do wrong!
Clear your cloudy mind and drench it with rain.
Smudge sage on your aura and let go of the pain.
Blow battles of bullying out of your head,
And forget all the stuff that has been said!
Forgive and start to live!

That poem, which I wrote long ago and often recite, emerged from a time of profound betrayal – a wound so deep it left me carrying the weight of hurt for years. Once I realised hanging on to hurt was not helpful to me – there was no possibility of further dialogue with the person in question – that 'forgiveness' poem became my little healing mantra. It offered solace to me and others who were seeking forgiveness or struggling to give it. Written two decades ago, it's a reminder of my own healing process. In my journey, I've learnt that forgiveness holds the key to my freedom. Embracing it again and again has been truly transformative.

I know genuine forgiveness isn't always possible. But when you can, try to let go: turn the other cheek and forgive. Remember, no matter how badly you were treated, that person was probably repeating a pattern and projecting their own pain and past hurts onto you. Send them compassion and bless their journey. It's all we can do.

To support your path toward forgiveness (again, where possible), here are a few prompts to help you reflect on your pain and help you release it.

♥   *What specific action or situation caused you this pain? How did this experience affect your life and relationships?*

♥ *What emotions are you feeling about this situation: anger, sadness, betrayal? (Do a web search for a feelings wheel if it's hard to find the right words.)*

♥ *What might have motivated the other person to act toward you in the hurtful way they did?*

♥ *Can you see their perspective, even if you don't agree with it?*

♥ *Is there any chance you can clear the air – communicate the hurt you have been feeling? Are you ready to forgive? Why or why not?*

♥ *How will you feel once you've forgiven?*

Ritual of release – when you cannot clear the air directly

While forgiveness is not always possible, when it is, it opens the door to healing, allowing you to loosen pain's grip before it consumes you.

- **Write a letter –** whether to someone else or yourself – that lets those emotions pour out. Choose a memory or event that still holds weight and let it all spill onto the page. Connect wholeheartedly with the situation, share your truth. Maybe this is as far as you can go, and this letter is a way for you to understand or acknowledge the hurt. But if it feels right, include some forgiveness. Write freely, with no judgement or filters.

- **Burn the letter.** Once you've written your letter, take a moment to read it aloud, if you can – or say it quietly to yourself. Then safely burn it as a symbolic act of release. Reflect on what it feels like to let go. This ritual can be a powerful tool for personal healing and emotional release, helping you move forward with greater clarity and peace. You absolutely deserve it!

• • •

Forgiveness, I've come to realise, isn't about forgetting, excusing, or letting the other person off the hook – it's about loosening the grip of the pain you've carried within yourself. It's a quiet, tender surrender that doesn't erase what happened, but it does make the burden lighter, and it also sweeps debris off the path ahead.

I know the process of forgiveness isn't straightforward: some days it feels impossible to achieve. But every time you choose to forgive, you're not just freeing the other person; you're freeing yourself. You're reaching for the peace that comes when you no longer let past wrongs control your present. This kind of healing is an act of grace toward yourself, and when you make space for it, you open your heart to more light.

Accountability

May you own your choices, come what may,
No excuses, no games, no delay.

It's truly admirable when someone has the courage to recognise their patterns, own their mistakes, and take responsibility for their actions. It's no small feat to name a behaviour, apologise sincerely, or work toward meaningful change. While you can't control how others show up, you can absolutely take charge of the energy, ripples, and frequency you put out into the world – and that's powerful.

I learnt this firsthand with my beautiful sister, Lize. Despite our deep love and connection, we occasionally found ourselves locked in hurtful clashes. It wasn't easy, but when I took a step back to acknowledge my role and disrupt some of the unhelpful patterns I was bringing to the table, something magical happened. Our dynamic shifted. Slowly but surely, things began to feel lighter, more aligned, and ultimately more loving. Of course, this wasn't a solo effort: Lize was also taking accountability for her contributions. Together, we grew, and I couldn't be prouder of us. Love you to bits, Lize!

The lesson? Accountability is one of the cornerstones of emotional intelligence. When you clean up your side of the street, everything else seems to rise with it. If you find yourself stuck in blame or struggling to see your part in a situation, here are some reflective questions to get you into a more accountable state:

♥ *What recent situation made you realise the importance of owning your actions?*

♥ How do you hold yourself accountable? Is there someone in your life that holds a clear mirror up to you and gives you feedback when you're not accountable?

♥ In what ways do you think your actions affect those around you? Where are you blaming another person and taking zero accountability?

♥ How do you respond when you recognise a mistake you've made?

♥ What fears or challenges do you face when it comes to being accountable?

Stretch your accountability muscles

Identify three areas of your life where you want to take accountability this month, reflecting on the impact your choices have on others. Choose someone to share these goals with to help support your journey. Let's take action and make a positive difference!

-
-
-

• • •

Stepping into accountability is like donning a superhero cape with a sparkly 'I Own My Mistakes' badge! It's not about being perfect but admitting when you've turned a molehill into a mountain. Every time you own up, imagine a tiny confetti cannon celebrating your growth. Being accountable isn't just about fixing things; it creates a ripple of honesty and connection. So, grab that cape, embrace your inner hero, and sprinkle some accountability magic! Take the leap and fly – and *be* fly!

Empathy

Empathy is hearing the echoes inside,
Of another's heart, where their feelings reside.
Then compassion may bloom, and you find a way –
An action, a gesture – to brighten their day.

Alrighty, divine you, let's move into some powerful work on empathy. It's a muscle we all need to strengthen, and one of the attributes of an emotionally intelligent person is that they have excellent empathy. Having empathy isn't just about understanding someone; it's more like the ability to imaginatively step into their shoes, feeling their world as if it were your own. That's a lot of what we mean when we talk about 'holding space' for someone: we take stock of their feelings in our internal deliberations.

There have been times when my own struggles – anger, hurt, and overwhelming emotions – made empathy feel like a distant dream. But every challenge has shaped me, expanding my ability to hold space for others with a deeper, more open heart. You know the feeling when you've walked through the fire, emerged stronger, and suddenly you're better able to connect with others in their own struggles? That's the gift of empathy: sometimes you have to experience the depths of yourself to truly understand what it means to be there for others and now, you have a chance to elevate that empathy even further.

MAPPING EMPATHY TO BRING IT TO LIFE
Call to mind someone in your life that you want to understand better. It could be a friend, family member, or a person you've had conflict with.

Find a quiet space. Close your eyes and take a few deep breaths. Imagine being in their shoes, living their life, carrying their emotions.

♥   *What's possibly driving their thoughts and feelings? Consider their personal situation, work stress, family dynamics, or anything else that might be shaping their current experience.*

♥   *What are they feeling? Anxiety? Joy? Overwhelm? Get specific when naming the emotions you imagine they're experiencing.*

♥   *How might their thoughts and feelings be affecting their actions? Note any behaviours you suspect are reflecting their emotional state. Are they shutting people out? Being extra talkative?*

♥   *Take a step back. Now that you are considering the full picture, can you feel more empathy? Is this exercise challenging your previous assumptions? This is where you see if you've been projecting your own feelings onto this person.*

♥   *Look for themes. Do you often misunderstand this person? Are there moments when your own experiences colour how you perceive them? Identify recurring challenges in your interactions.*

♥   *After a week or two, revisit this map. Have things shifted in your relationship? How has your empathy deepened your connection?*

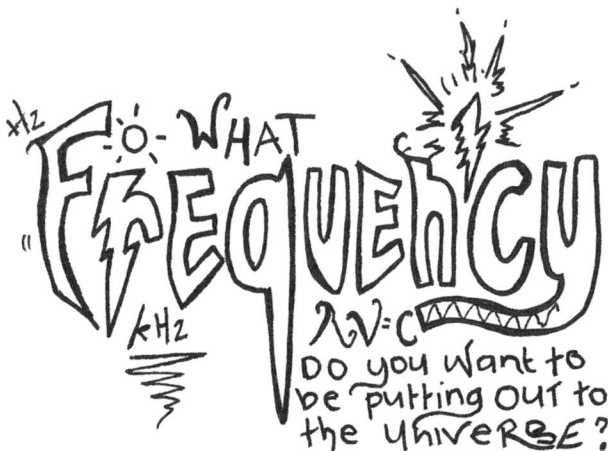

WHAT FREQUENCY kHz $\lambda \nu = c$ DO you want to be putting out to the uhiveRSE?

RADICAL EMPATHY – FOR THE EXTRA KEEN!

This one's next-level empathy, gorgeous. Imagine fully entering someone else's emotional world: no judgements, just understanding. Radical empathy allows you to *feel* with someone in a way that transforms both of you. It's not just listening; it's embodying their experience. When you meet people here, your relationships change forever.

Here are some journal prompts for if you're willing to look into radical empathy and emotional contagion:

♥ *Reflect on a time when you felt truly understood by someone. How did their empathy impact your feelings or actions? How can you replicate that experience for someone else?*

♥ *In your next conversation, commit to listening without judgement. What does that feel like for you? How might this change the dynamic of your interaction?*

♥   Consider any preconceived notions you have about others' experiences. How can you work to set these aside to create a deeper connection with someone you might have misunderstood?

♥   Think of a recent moment when someone shared their struggles with you. Revisit that memory like a video that you can replay bits of. How did you respond? Edit the video so that you approach that conversation with radical empathy instead. What does it look like now?

• • •

Think about moments when you've felt emotions similar to what others are experiencing. When my friends are going through heartbreak, a deep loss, or are feeling stuck and unsure how to move forward, I truly understand. I've been in those spaces myself. But I know how much it means to feel fully seen and understood, without judgement or having solutions thrust at me. It's not the time to share my own experiences – unless asked to. Sharing my story can unintentionally shift the focus away from their feelings and the moment they're in. Instead, I focus on holding space with as much empathy and presence as possible – because that's what we all need most in those vulnerable times.

Compassion

Compassion is love in action.

While empathy allows you to connect and understand another emotionally and share in their feelings, compassion drives you to take action and help. Make compassion a passion: let's get it in fashion! (Ummm ... Okay, Lu, ya big rhyming dork!)

Compassion is about rolling our sleeves up to make a difference – to lighten the load of another's struggle. Maybe it's calling your friend every couple of days to check in or helping them navigate 'that thing'. You're not necessarily aiming to fix everything, but find a way to make a contribution, whether in deeds or words.

Though don't forget, taking action is not always the way to go when someone is in pain. Simply being present, seeing another – empathy – is sometimes enough. So, yeah, tune in ... perhaps ask the person you care about what would be most helpful for them right now.

Compassion entails offering support without judgement. It means accepting others' feelings and experiences as they are, without criticism, and fostering a safe and trusting environment where individuals feel valued and understood.

♥ *Think of a time when someone came to you for support. How did you respond? Were you able to provide non-judgemental support? If not, what could you do differently next time to create a more accepting space?*

♥ *Identify a relationship in your life that could benefit from more compassion from you specifically. What precise actions or gestures can you take to show more kindness and care toward this person? How might this enhance your relationship?*

♥ *How do you show yourself compassion? What commitment could you make to do more of this?*

• • •

Compassion is a transformative force that not only deepens your connections but also nurtures your own heart. Every act of kindness creates ripples that uplift others and your own journey. If you're ever down in the dumps yourself, go do something compassionate for someone and see how that depression lifts in you. It's magical!

Parenthood

May your heart be light,
Through every challenge, hold tight,
You're doing more than alright!

I proudly call myself an 'earth mumma'. While I have not birthed children of my own in this lifetime, I'm surrounded by kids who I care for and love as much as I can. I wholeheartedly believe that children are our future and that it takes a village to raise kids. All parents need a crew of committed adults pouring love and support into their children. The mental load and the juggle of parenthood is so massive that every contribution helps. Kids can get a huge kick out of being able to chat comfortably with another adult. Here's to lifting, loving, and nurturing the next generation!

I've been a stepmum (or 'spare-ent', as I like to say); and I am a godmum, an aunty, a daughter, and have taught and supported countless kids in drama; also, I've been very blessed to have supported three births as a doula. My love for children is really genuine. I just love them all. I'm a bit of a big kid myself in many ways. I've also had my share of grieving over not becoming a mother. My dream is to meet a partner with kids, and one day become a granny. I'd love that.

To all the wonderful parents out there: thank you for all the sacrifices you make, doing your best with the resources you have. May you and your children flourish, and may your bond be filled with respect and adoration for one another. Participating in this guided journal is a remarkable commitment – one that will nurture not only your own wellbeing but – by osmosis – that of your beautiful children, too. Let's prioritise being role models and growing our children into emotionally intelligent humans – the planet could really do with more folk getting around like that.

A couple of questions for parents to ponder:

♥   How do you show up as your best self for your child, even when you're feeling overwhelmed or imperfect?

♥   What are the deeper needs behind your child's behaviour, and how can you respond with empathy rather than frustration?

♥ *How are you nurturing your own wellbeing so that you can be present and available to support your child's emotional growth?*

♥ *How do you want to show up as a parent?*

SHINE YOUR LIGHT

Dear Lu,

I've got young kids and am often unable to sneak away and have 'me time'. What would you suggest to help when I'm feeling overwhelmed, anxious, and/or frustrated?

Hey ya, beautiful mumma,

Parenting is indeed relentless, and while I don't walk in your shoes, I deeply admire your dedication. As a passionate village aunt, I've witnessed the tireless efforts of parents and understand the importance of carving out moments for yourself. Here are some suggestions to help you find balance and relief:

Prioritise self-care: Dedicate self-care time that is non-negotiable. Whether it's a yoga session, a run, or simply reading a book with a cup of tea, find what nourishes you and make it a regular part of your week. This time is crucial for recharging your spirit.

Weave in small moments: When a larger block of time isn't possible, look for smaller pockets of self-care throughout your day. Even a few minutes of deep breathing, a quick meditation, or enjoying a moment of solitude in the bathroom can offer a reset.

Enlist support: Consider who can support you in carving out this time. Is there a partner, family member, or friend who can help with the kids so you can take a break? Sometimes, asking for help is a vital part of self-care.

Make conscious choices: Reflect on your daily activities and see where you might make adjustments. For instance, could you reduce TV time and replace it with a soothing bath or a nourishing podcast? Every choice you make contributes to your overall wellbeing.

Set boundaries: Fiercely guard your self-care time. Communicate with those around you about the importance of these moments for your wellbeing. It's okay to set limits to ensure you get the time you need.

Embrace flexibility: Understand that self-care might look different on different days. There's not always time for a full yoga class followed by meditation, but maybe savouring that chai latte to go will put extra sparkle in your day. Be flexible with yourself and adapt your practices based on what you can manage at the moment.

Remember, the choices you make for your wellbeing ultimately benefit your family, too. By taking care of yourself, you become a more balanced and inspired parent.

Sending you strength and support,

X Lu

• • •

To every parent reading this: all the love you give your children, every last bit of effort, and even your moments of doubt, are all worth it. You're shaping lives, nurturing futures, and weaving a legacy of care to the best of your ability, even in the chaos. Parenting isn't about perfection – it's about presence, patience, and the courage to keep showing up.

May this chapter also remind you that *your* wellbeing is just as important as how much love and attention you pour into your children (it's okay to leave the dishes in the sink once in a while). You're the heartbeat of your family, and when you thrive, your children will flourish, too. Wishing you smooth sailing on the good ship *Parenthood*!

Family

Family's where love and chaos collide,
Where tolerance and empathy must both reside.
Through conflict and care, we grow and we learn,
Grateful for lessons that forever return!

How are your family relationships these days? Do you eagerly anticipate those big gatherings, like Christmas? Maybe you've got a family member who truly gets you, or perhaps your circle looks different now, with soul family filling the space. Family dynamics can be like an emotional maze – complex, messy, and full of unexpected turns. While handling these relationships can be challenging, they also offer some of the deepest opportunities for growth and self-discovery.

Not everyone gets to work through their 'family stuff' with their actual family, and sometimes the kindest, healthiest choice is to step away completely or grieve the family you came from and never knew. Even families that seem picture-perfect from the outside have their troubles. No matter your situation, know you're not alone in figuring it all out – it's a universal human experience.

Family ties are woven with deep histories, often stirring up a whirlwind of emotions or even sending us back into old childhood regressions. I've learnt that forgiveness and letting go are two of the most freeing gifts I can give myself. Of course, there are times when the wounds feel too fresh, and my ego stubbornly holds onto the pain. In those moments, seeking the right professional support or turning to a transformative book can help shift my perspective and gently pull me out of my story, guiding me toward healing with more grace.

My family journey has been a wild roller-coaster – filled with connection, pain, and plenty of beautiful rewards. Sure, conflicts have left their marks, but I've realised that those clashes often hold the keys to unique insights. That old saying, 'If you think you're enlightened, spend a week with your family', couldn't ring truer! Shared histories have a way of reopening old wounds, but if you're willing to dig deep, more understanding of yourself and family members awaits.

Taking ownership of my role in family dynamics has been a game-changer. It's meant getting honest about my part in past conflicts (so righteous at times ... gulp!) and offering forgiveness – to myself and said family members – and letting things go. Checking in with myself about my actions has been key. I try to remember that we're all just doing the best we can with the tools we've got. That said, wow, it can be tough work sometimes being so accountable. Crikey!

Given you're doing the work of self-reflecting through these pages, I truly believe you're one of the change-makers in your family. You're the highest evolutionary expression of your ancestors – the one they've been waiting for – armed with the awareness, knowledge, and resources to break old patterns and build healthier, more vibrant legacies. We're living in a remarkable time, with access to transformative healing tools and communities that support growth like never before. How inspiring is that?

My hope for you is that you find harmony and acceptance, not just within your family, but in all kinds of connections – whether they are by blood or by choice. And hey, if stepping back and embracing some solo time is what you need, get in there! Love doesn't have rules, and sometimes the relationships that matter most fit in the palm of your hand ... or come with fins, feathers, or a wagging tail!

May your journey with family be filled with love, growth, and healing. You are deeply loved by the Earth and the Universe, always.

Here are a few questions to reflect on, but remember: family dynamics can be a sensitive topic, so be kind to yourself. Wrap your heart in some soothing metaphorical balm while you explore. You've got this!

♥ *How do you feel about your family dynamics? Are there specific relationships that bring you joy or perhaps some that feel more complicated? Take a moment to explore how your family connections impact you emotionally.*

♥ *What role do you play in your family's story? Have you noticed any patterns or recurring themes in your interactions with family? How have you contributed to these dynamics, and where can you take ownership and make changes?*

♥   *What does forgiveness look like for you in your family? Are there wounds that still feel raw, and how might forgiveness (of yourself or others) free you from the grip of those past experiences? What would it take for you to let go of old hurts?*

♥   *When faced with family conflict, what tools do you rely on to stay grounded? Do you have a strategy to navigate family stress? Maybe it's turning to support, reading a book, or taking a break — what helps you restore balance in those moments?*

♥   *What kind of legacy do you want to build within your family? How can you break old patterns and create healthier, more vibrant connections in your family going forward? Consider what positive change you wish to contribute to your family's future.*

Dear Lu,

About eight years ago, I found my parents' behaviour so toxic that I cut off communication. Now I feel ready to reconnect. What would your advice be?

Estranged son

G'day, legend!

Reconnecting with your parents after almost a decade is a significant and courageous step. It's essential to approach this journey with self-care, low expectations, and mindful preparation. Here are some thoughts that may help:

Stay grounded: Remember that your worth and value come from within. You have grown into a resilient and self-aware individual. Embrace the person you are today and hold on to that inner strength as you navigate this reunion.

Manage expectations: Healing and rebuilding relationships takes time. Understand that not everything will be resolved immediately (of at all), and that's okay. Patience and compassion toward yourself and your parents will be key.

Practise forgiveness: Keep an open heart and remember that your parents likely did their best with the tools they had. They, too, were shaped by their experiences and may have grown in their own ways. Embrace a forgiving mindset, which can help you in moving forward together. It may turn out that the kindest thing to do is sever the tie and re-create a new soul family for your life, but where you can, practise forgiveness.

Establish boundaries: If you're all still willing to keep trying – protect your emotional wellbeing, think about what boundaries you need. Listen to their boundaries. Clearly and kindly communicate these boundaries to your parents. It might help to write them down and rehearse how you'll express them, ensuring that they are respected during your interactions.

Take it slow: There's no rush in this process. Allow the reconnection to develop naturally, taking small steps and giving yourself time to adjust. Your emotional safety is paramount, and pacing yourself will help maintain your wellbeing.

Self-compassion: Be kind to yourself throughout this journey. It's okay to have mixed emotions and to need time to process them. Lean on your support system, whether friends, a therapist, or a community that understands your situation.

Remember, this reconnection is a testament to your growth and strength. Trust in your ability to navigate this path with grace and courage.

Warmly,
X Lu

• • •

You're a joy – ships ahoy! The inconvenient truth is, sometimes you might feel like the lone sailor navigating the stormy seas of your family dynamics. Hey: it is what it is. Often, your knowledge, acknowledgement, humility, forgiveness, and acceptance are all that's needed to spark a ripple effect, inspiring others to shift, too. Set your bearings and hold steady; role-model what it means to be a compassionate family member; and watch as others might just meet you there. All aboard, and best of luck!

Singles

In the dance of solitude, you find your grace,
Secure in yourself, you move at your own pace.

I actually really cherish and love being single. I learnt a long time ago to savour and enjoy my own company, and I never really feel lonely. It's transformational being at peace with that mindset. Even if I spend the rest of this lifetime without a partner, I will continue to find ways to keep my heart full and happy.

Having a 'lone wolf' side allows me to move between the worlds of connection and solitude. I enjoy the freedom and space for silence, creativity, and self-discovery. I'm open to meeting my life-long partner when the time is right, but I feel at peace in this chapter, embracing everything it has to offer: there is so much. This balance lets me celebrate my independence while staying open to future love, trusting that each experience is shaping me into who I'm meant to be.

I also find joy in knowing I've mastered the art of being single: whoever steps into my life now will feel truly right, not as a necessity. I don't need someone to 'complete me' but I'd love to be in a relationship with someone who adds richness to my already fulfilled world. No dependency, just two people adding value to each other's lives in the most beautiful way.

These journal prompts are for the single folk among us.

♥   *How do you currently perceive solitude in your life? Do you see it as a privilege or a burden?*

♥   What activities truly nourish your soul, and how can you incorporate them into your solitary time?

♥   What qualities do you appreciate about yourself that make your own company enjoyable?

♥ *How do you handle unprocessed emotions when they arise in solitude?*
What tools do you have to support your healing process?

♥ *What are the pros and cons of being single?*

• • •

Aloneness is not a state of lacking but a state of completeness within oneself. If you're single, let that light shine brilliantly! Being single is your chance to sparkle unapologetically and illuminate the world uncompromisingly. Single isn't a waiting room; it's a whole vibe – freedom, peace, and the joy of being complete just as you are. Victory lap!

Free Flow Here...

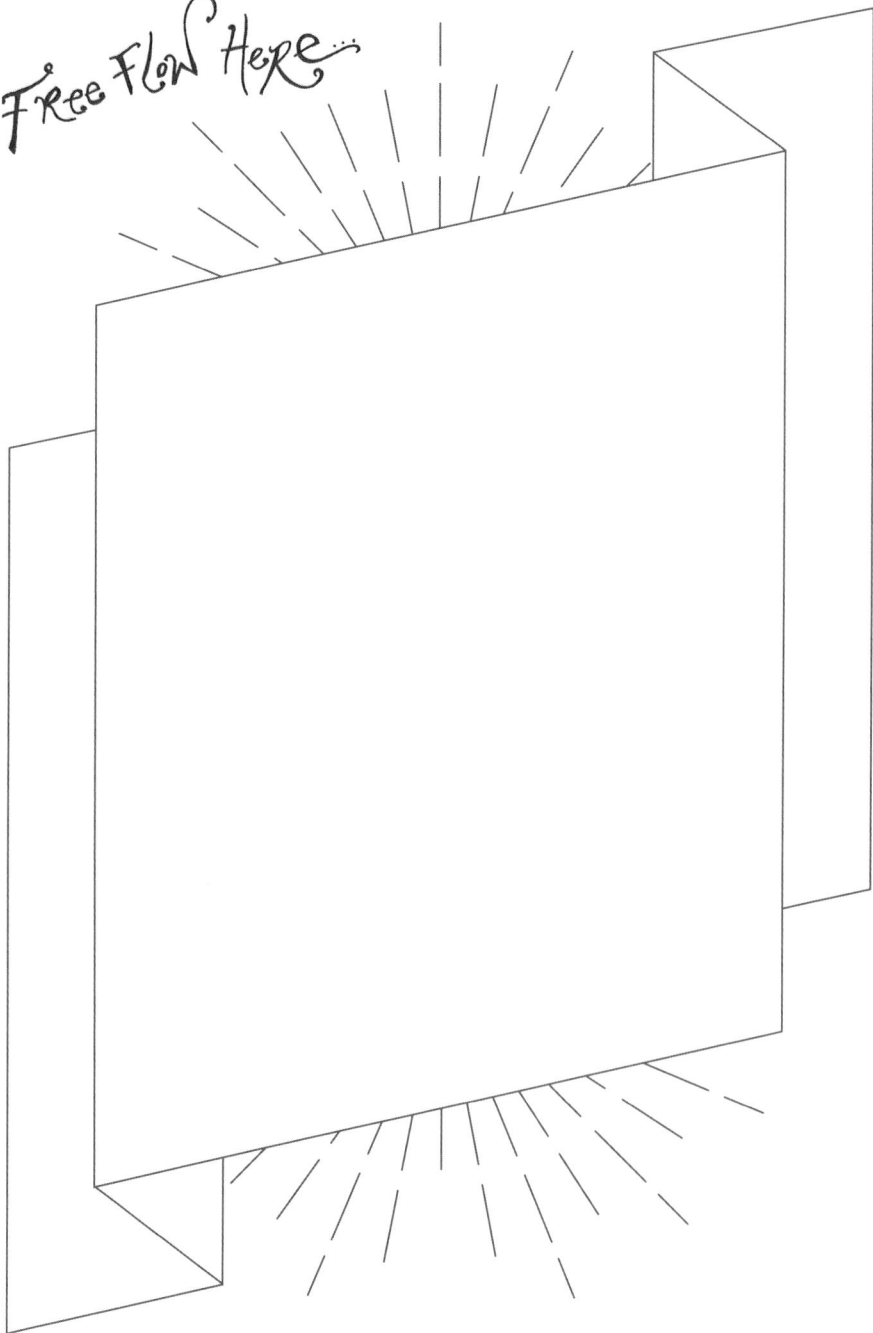

Dating

First date, nerves collide,
I spill my drink, but do we still jive?
Is it love or just the wine?
Guess we'll see, let's give it time ...

Get ready to elevate your dating game with these bold, cheeky, and empowering tips for navigating the wild world of modern romance! Step one? Commit to showing up and taking inspired action – because, let's face it, love won't come knocking if you're not making moves. Your effort truly matters, and these tips are here as your loving reminders – guiding principles designed to help you attract and nurture the partnership of your dreams.

I picked up most of these while hosting 'Soulful Speed Dating' – and while dating – so take what resonates, forgive yourself if you miss a few, and, of course, remember authenticity is key. Happy dating, you fabulous sparkle of emotionally intelligent magic!

Be yourself.
No games: just be honest and up front. There's nothing more attractive than being unapologetically you. Ditch finding the 'right fit' – just dress to impress yourself; wear what makes you feel amazing. Show up fabulous as you are and let that natural charm shine.

Confidence is sexy.
Walk in knowing your worth. Don't be shy to take the lead – take charge and suggest something fun. Confidence isn't just attractive, it's contagious.

Be mindful of body language.
Open posture – the body never lies. Smile. And eyes, darling. Keep eye contact for an instant spark of connection. Windows to the soul and all that!

Curiosity is key.
Ask about their passions, dig into their dreams, and lean in. Nothing says, 'I'm into you' like genuine interest. And, hey: really listen up. Give them your full attention, like they're the best Netflix show you've ever seen.

Open mind, open heart.
Try not to shut down different views. Keep your mind wide open; you just might learn something!

Respect boundaries.
Different comfort zones, different strokes: read the room. Don't push! Your respect for their boundaries makes you even more lovable.

Positive vibes only.
No one wants a gloomy date; this is no time for touchy topics. Keep the convo light, leave complaints at home, and sprinkle in a few laughs. Keep ex-talk on the back burner – save that for later dates. This is fun time!

Plan with passion.
Not all dates have to happen in restaurants. Make it memorable. Trying something new together? Yes, please! Plan a date you'll both enjoy – then let the spontaneity flow!

Fashionably punctual.
Show you're serious by being on time. Don't keep 'em waiting – unless you're fashionably late with a good story, accidentally!

Stay present.

If drinking, sip – don't guzzle – and know your limits! Ditch distractions, especially that phone! Nothing beats a present, focused date.

Manners matter.

'Please', 'Excuse me': small words with a big impact. Expressing your appreciation with a heartfelt 'thank you' goes a long way, too (no gushing; keep it cool and classy). Good manners are the real charm!

Take it slow.

There's no rushing good romance! Let the magic unfold at its own pace. Patience is a virtue; connections take time. Let things unfold naturally.

Adapt and flow.

Plans change? Go with it. Show your easy-going side! Awkward silence? Ask an open-ended question or share something fun! Always expect the unexpected. Not every date will be 'the one', and that's fine!

Go easy on yourself.

Every date's a new experience. Let go of perfectionism and enjoy the moment.

Unleash your humour.

There's nothing more bonding than a laugh. If you've got a sense of humour, use it! Laugh at yourself, too. A little self-deprecation is disarming.

Unleash your inner kid.

Be playful, embrace your inner quirks – let that little weirdo inside you shine – and watch how the fun doubles.

Flirt and tease lightly.

Playful banter is key. Just keep it light and respectful – flirt like a pro!

Know your worth.

No 'settling' allowed. If they're not a gem, don't force it. But do say no with style: keep it kind but straightforward.

Rejection is redirection.

If it's a no, that's A-okay! Keep it light and keep it moving.

Respect.

Never tolerate disrespect. Your worth is undeniable.

Let your sass shine, your confidence radiate, and enjoy every moment of this dating adventure. You're more than enough, and with these tips, you're unstoppable!

• • •

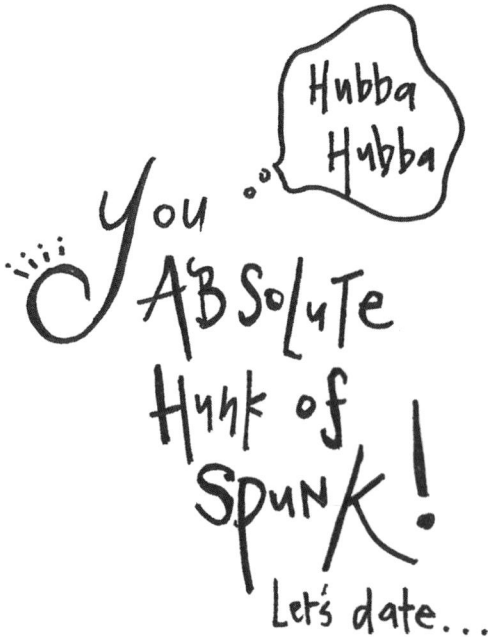

Alrighty: you might want some questions for your date, too, so I've plonked in here a mix of sassy, silly, and serious questions. You pick a few or – even better – trust yourself. These are just to inspire! A couple to pop up your sleeve. Now, go get 'em, tiger!

'What's something you're really passionate about that lights you up – the thing you could talk about for hours?' Or, 'What brings you the most joy in your daily life?'

'If you could give your younger self one piece of advice, what would it be?' Or, 'What's a mistake you're secretly glad you made because it taught you something epic?'

'What's your favourite way to spend a free day – and does it involve being social or solo?' Or, 'If you had to give your life a hashtag right now, what would it be?'

'What's a quality you value most in relationships, whether romantic or platonic?' Or, 'What's a personality trait in someone else that makes you go, "Yep, you're my people"?'

'What's the most ridiculous trend you've ever fallen for? (Please don't say Crocs with socks.)' Or, 'What's your most ridiculous "This only happens to me" moment? I want full details.'

• • •

I know, that was a lot to take in! But think of it as a treasure trove of reminders – little nudges to help guide you. Above all else, though, be your unique self. What you express should resonate with the other person; if it doesn't, it just means they're not your right fit. You gave that audition your best shot; now it's over. Time to move on. And whatever you do, don't give up! Keep shining your light! Happy dating, you delightfully datable wonder!

Hey, gorgeous lady!

As we grow emotionally, we become more discerning about the company we keep, and that can make finding the right relationship feel a little trickier. But here's the thing: you're no longer willing to settle for less than what you deserve. You've got the wisdom to recognise what emotionally unavailable looks like – and you want the complete opposite. And honestly? You've earnt that.

My advice: keep growing your emotional intelligence and take action to connect with like-minded people. Find places where emotionally aware folks hang out – whether that's workshops, online communities, or even local hiking or book clubs. Be brave and get to know potential suitors who are also in alignment with your values.

As you tidy up your inner world, you'll begin to attract people who meet you at that frequency. Keep sharpening your self-awareness, grow from your strengths and weaknesses, and be honest and kind in all your communications. Practise empathy, and model the emotional intelligence that you can be proud of.

Keep growing, keep evolving and keep leading by example. Stay committed to your intention, because the person you're looking for is out there. Don't give up – just keep doing your inner work, and above all, make sure to have fun along the way!

X Lu

Intimate Partnership

In the intimacy of two souls, you are born anew
In love's embrace, you are safe to be true

I've had the privilege of sharing deep, intimate relationships with extraordinary people, each one peeling back new layers of who I am. These connections have allowed me to discover uncharted depths within myself. While each experience has been heart-opening, they've also been bittersweet. At some point, every one of my intimate relationships has ended, and saying goodbye is never easy.

Intimate partnerships are beautiful but seldom simple. More often than not, they act as mirrors, showing us both our strengths and vulnerabilities. They help you uncover the kind of energy you want to invite into your life and the things that need to be released. For instance, you might find yourself with a passionate mountain biker eager to explore the outdoors every weekend, while what you long for is a quiet time at the theatre, or losing yourself in a good book.

Relationships require hard work: setting aside the ego, embracing vulnerability, and navigating the emotional ups and downs of love, rejection, and each other's uniqueness, not to mention the compromises in terms of meshing schedules, social circles, and so on. Falling deeply in love can shake the foundations of our identity, forcing us to shed old parts of ourselves and grow into something new. Shall we get into it with some inquiry?

Reflecting on your current intimate partnership

Below are some great questions to ask each other in a quiet and sacred moment together. It's so good to come back to centre together and ensure you're on the right track. Ask your partner, or each other, the following:

♥   *What's something that I do that makes you feel truly seen and loved, and how can I do more of it?*

♥   *Are there ways I can support you better in your personal growth or dreams?*

♥   *What's a challenge we've faced that makes you feel proud of us for overcoming together?*

♥   *When you imagine our future together, what excites you the most?*

Reflecting on past relationships (Gulp!)

Thinking through past relationships can feel like prodding at a sore spot, hoping it won't hurt anymore. You're safe here, this is your place! Rather than merely poking at wounds, though, let's uncover valuable lessons to carry forward. Noting what worked, what didn't, and any recurring patterns helps avoid repeating past mistakes. This is a bit of free flow, yo!

♥ *List five cherished aspects from your last significant relationship.*

-
-
-
-
-

♥ *In what ways did you evolve during this relationship? Write down five deep lessons you learnt. As you call these to mind, savour the moments that resonated.*

-

-

-

-

-

♥   What boundaries did you discover within yourself in this dynamic? How did you learn to express your needs and desires more clearly?

♥   Did your partner challenge your beliefs or perspectives?

♥   How did your capacity for empathy grow through this relationship?

♥   During difficult times, what new coping strategies did you develop?

As you reflect on your growth through intimate relationships, ask yourself:

♥   *Would you date you?*

♥   *If not, why not?*

♥   *If yes, why?*

♥   *What areas still call for evolution?*

• • •

This isn't about self-criticism but an opportunity to inspire deeper love within yourself – whether for a future partner, the one by your side today, and/or for you, gorgeous. Here's to all forms of intimate partnership and the profound lessons and love that they invite you to explore. The sky's the limit – woohoo!

Dear utterly divine you!

Although I don't have a physical disability, in 2018, I was bed-bound for eight months with a severely debilitated back.

Passion comes from within, and it's essential to cultivate it, regardless of your circumstances. If you had passion before, in order to rekindle it, you'll need to put on your creative hat and look beyond your limitations. Take full responsibility for reactivating every chakra, from Muladhara (your base) to Sahasrara (Crown).

Adaptation is one of humanity's greatest qualities. Take stock of your circumstances and find ways to be flexible. Work first on you: discover new hobbies and interests that align with your abilities and stir passion within you.

Redefine in your own terms what intimacy looks like. Remove the pressure of expectation and explore new expressions through communication, touch, cuddles, and shared activities. Find joy in fun, creative expressions of love.

Research inspiring individuals with physical disabilities who have navigated their paths with grace and passion. Learn from their journeys. Find peace within your situation, and seek professional help when needed.

Remember, you hold the codes to your passion. Keep exploring, adapting and embracing life's possibilities.

All the best
X Lu

Separating

Paths now split, hearts ache,
Respectful goodbyes, love's soft break.

Break-ups – whether romantic or platonic – are sad and stressful. Too many relationships end in conflict, hurt, and trauma, leaving a deep wound, especially when it's someone you've loved fully. When children, pets, or shared assets are involved, the situation can become even more complicated.

This is a tribute to the process of separating, or conscious uncoupling, with kindness, empathy, and respect. The more consciously each person can approach the end of a chapter, the more beneficial it is for their nervous system's state, both leading up to and during the break-up – and well after. The ideal is to stay grounded, prioritise self-care, and keep compassion flowing. While not easy, doing so honours the love that was shared and the necessary timing for both of you to move on. I know it may not always be possible, but if it is, here are some questions to ask yourself:

♥   *How can I stay grounded and preserve my peace in this situation?*

♥   *What is one thing I can do right now to take care of myself during this time?*

♥   *In what ways am I still holding on to this relationship, and what would it feel like to let go with compassion?*

And here are some questions for the person you are saying goodbye to. Perhaps you want to ask each other these while partaking in active listening. Find a dedicated time that works for both of you, create a sacred space to be in each other's company, and ask each other:

♥ *How can we ensure that we part with kindness and respect?*

♥ *What has been the most important part of this relationship and how can we honour that in its ending?*

♥ *Is there anything left unsaid or unresolved that we should address before moving forward?*

♥ *How can we support each other in transitioning to a new chapter?*

• • •

And so, with that, honour yourself and each other for all that you've learnt and shared. Bow to the challenges, the effort, the co-creation, and the moments of joy along the way. Acknowledge the grace it takes to let go with dignity and love. May you strive to do the least harm and leave each other better than you found one another. My prayer is that your relationship has nurtured growth in you and that you're now – or soon – ready to embrace the freedom to spread your new wings anew. Lift-off!

Hi Lu

In relationships, it's easier to see your partner's faults and blame them, but how do you see what part you are playing and where you are going wrong?

Hey there, lovely

I feel like a bit of an imposter answering this, since I'm not currently in a relationship. However, I have a lot of experience with this topic and will strive to figure it out better in my next relationship.

It's so true, isn't it? It's often easier to blame and shame and point outward rather than look within. Owning our part can be challenging – seeing our shadows, our wounds, our victim mentality and our projections. Intimate relationships hold the biggest mirror up to us; everything shows up when we're travelling alongside each other in a partnership. It can be hard, but the opportunity for growth is immense.

The foundation of emotional intelligence is self-awareness. We need to cultivate this as our base while forgiving ourselves and each other for all our human imperfections. None of us are perfect, and we've all been parented, socialised, and traumatised in different ways. Holding radical kindness and acceptance for others, as well as for ourselves, is crucial. It's important that boundaries are reciprocally respected.

Keep checking yourself and your motivations and intentions. Check in with your inner manipulator (we all have one) and get curious about the dynamics playing out. Ask yourself questions like: Why are we triggering each other in moments? Why are you feeling frustrated and unregulated? Where in the dynamic are you feeling unheard, and where are you not hearing them?

Remember, your triggers often reveal what you haven't owned, worked through, or resolved. Look at them and get curious. I know it's not easy. Keep being accountable, and humble yourself to work toward a good outcome for both of you, rather than needing to be right.

Try journalling about your strengths and weaknesses. When do you get frustrated? Why? What's at the heart of it? Did you feel like this as a kid? Get curious about your core wounds and your partner's, and try to find peace on your journey together. It might take a couple of years with a couples' psychologist/counsellor, if that's possible, or you can do your own work and research. See this as an opportunity to grow. Easier said than done, I know. You're courageous in asking and are ready to make the shift.

And, so it is.

All the best!
X Lu

Maintaining Relationships

When you tend to your bonds and keep them strong,
Relationship roots grow deep and long.

As beautifully imperfect social beings, we thrive on connections, and investing time and love into our relationships is one of the best ways to use our energy. Can I get a 'heavens, yeah!'? (In my mind, a thunderous 'HEAVENS, YEAH!' echoes through the Universe from out ya mouths in unison!) Here's a quick checklist to keep you focused on nurturing those important bonds.

Communication.
Foster open, empathetic dialogue. Figure out each other's love language: share yours and know what theirs is.

Quality time.
Prioritise shared experiences.

Honesty and trust.
Be transparent, consistent, and reliable.

Shared interests.
Cultivate shared hobbies and interests. Take an interest in their interests: even just listening is lovely. Hold space for their enthusiasm and passions.

Consider lifestyle factors.
Align on health and wellness priorities.

Express gratitude and affection.
Show appreciation and affection. Acknowledge and respect each other.

Compromise and flexibility.
Embrace adaptability and compromise.

Personal growth.
Support mutual personal growth. Grow together.

Face conflict.
Handle disagreements constructively; address them positively.

Be supportive.
Offer unwavering support and acceptance.

Build intimacy.
Foster emotional and physical closeness.

Keep things fresh.
Inject novelty to avoid monotony. Be unexpected in all the best ways.

Have fun. For the love of all that is good, HAVE FUN!

• • •

This list is just a starting point. But a commitment to open communication, mutual respect, and continuous growth is the foundation of any healthy relationship.

And let's not forget, even challenging relationships offer valuable lessons. Here's to you, to this wild and woolly human experience, and to the connections you weave along the way. May you find peace, joy, and understanding in the dazzling dance of relationships.

SHINE ON

Growth isn't a destination, it's the art of becoming – one step, trip, and triumph at a time. 'Future you' is a work in progress, constantly shaped by choices, learnings, and dreams.

This section is all about 'future you' – the version of yourself that's unfolding and evolving as we go through this process. The incredible thing about the growth journey is that it's limitless. You're constantly unwrapping new layers of your true self, and there's no final destination. I don't know about you, but I'd much rather be on the journey – taking each twist and turn, exploring the unknown – than simply arriving at a final 'point' (booooring!).

And here's something you know but – why not – I'll remind you again: the road isn't a straight path. It's cyclical, meaning that certain lessons will revisit you again and again. Every time they come around, you'll meet them with new insight, more wisdom, and a deeper understanding of yourself. That's how growth truly works. You don't just 'pass' the test once; you continue to evolve with each go-around, adding more tools to your emotional toolbox every time.

• • •

I recommend that you check in with yourself on a regular basis. Take a little pause to see where you're at and where you're headed. I promise it'll be worth the moment of reflection. Ask yourself what you have recently learnt about emotional intelligence. How is it showing up in your life? Are these insights impacting your relationships? Are you more aware, more present, more understanding? Are there any areas of emotional intelligence that might need a little more love? How do you picture these changes helping you as you go forward?

I'm also all about vibe checks – as in keeping the vibes high. Sometimes the best move is a quiet night in to recharge, and other times it's all about hitting the dancefloor and soaking up the energy of vibrant, fun-loving souls.

When I was on *Married at First Sight*, I had to keep my vibe game strong. It was tough at times, and I didn't want the challenges I faced to spill over onto my fellow castmates, who were mostly younger than me and having a tough time themselves. So, I leant into serious self-care and brought in a sprinkle of woo-woo magic and pragmatism to help me stay grounded and level up.

I've got a rotation of high-vibin' tips that can work wonders, depending on the situation. Use intuitively, you'll know what's for you. Ready to vibe higher? Check these out!

Disperse heavy energy. When you're overwhelmed by negative energy, visualise sending it back to the earth to be transformed. Get a little dramatic with it! Plant your hands on the ground and say, 'Thank you, earth, for emptying me of that energy!' Try it! How does it feel to release heavy vibes?

Tune into positive frequencies. Surround yourself with what lifts you up. Trust your instincts and seek out people and experiences that resonate or elevate your high vibe. What environments and people make you feel uplifted and energised?

Protect your energy. When you're in a busy, chaotic space, carry tools that help you stay centred – like a calming botanical, earthy spritz or your favourite playlist that is soothing for your soul (check out the ones I made for you on page 17). What grounding tool helps you feel calm and present in chaotic environments?

Send love and blessings. Picture your heart as a beacon of positive energy, sending out love to everyone and everything around you. Who can you send love and blessings to today? Send out those good vibes and cheer the world around you on!

Release what you can't control. There's freedom in letting go. Recognise what you can't change and release it. Focus on what you can control – your attitude, your energy, and your response. What's one thing you can let go of that no longer serves you today?

Engage in self-care. Self-care isn't selfish; it's necessary! Whether it's a bath, reading a good book, or practising your favourite hobby, give yourself permission to do something that nurtures your mind, body, and spirit. What self-care activity could you treat yourself to today?

Express gratitude. Gratitude is the ultimate vibe booster! Take a moment to reflect on the things you're thankful for, big or small. What are three things you're grateful for today? Write them down, let that gratitude fill you up.

Reframe negative situations. What if every challenge was a lesson in disguise? Next time something negative happens, try to see the opportunity for growth. How can you reframe a recent challenge into something that will serve you? It's like turning lemons into life lessons. Squeeze the bejesus outta those lemons!

• • •

I've come to see that ageing isn't something to fear – it's a privilege that many don't get to experience. Sure, there will come a time when it's all over, but until then, I want to keep learning, giving, and sharing everything I can. You? And eventually, there will be a time for stillness, too: a time to reflect, to soak in the wisdom of the years, and to savour the peace and contentment that comes from a life well lived.

It's been a true privilege to live, on and off, on my mum's beautiful land along the Great Ocean Road, witnessing how she embraces ageing with such grace and contentment. Now in her 70s, she continues to inspire me daily with her vibrant energy and positive outlook – she's proof that life can just keep getting better. Dad, too, is rocking his 70s, and they both remind me that there's always more to look forward to. I've started to refer to life as long, not short – a perspective that frees me from the anxiety of time running out. It helps me slow down, relax, and dream big for 'future me'.

Take a moment now to look ahead. The path you're on isn't a race; it's an ongoing, exciting evolution. You're not just moving toward a future – you're creating it, with every lesson you embrace and every new version of yourself you discover. Keep going, keep growing, and keep trusting the beautiful adventure that lies ahead. Here's a couple of future questions to keep ya rolling forward in celebration of all that you are – and are becoming:

♥ *What does future you look like? Take a moment to imagine yourself in five years. What qualities, habits, or accomplishments do you envision?*

♥ *Which lessons keep cycling back into your life? Can you identify any recurring themes or challenges? How might your fresh insights help you approach them differently this time?*

♥ What excites you most about your ongoing growth? What part of the adventure ahead fills you with hope or energy?

♥ How do you view ageing? Has your perspective on growing older shifted? How can you embrace it as a privilege and a part of your journey?

♥ What are you letting go of to make way for new thoughts, feelings, and possibilities ahead?

♥ *When life slows down one day, what will you cherish most? Looking far ahead, what memories, connections, or achievements do you hope to reflect on with pride and contentment?*

• • •

Letting go of past versions of ourselves can be bittersweet, but it's also beautiful. Embracing change with courage opens the door to the next iteration of who you are. Each step forward is part of the journey: meet the future you there with excitement! I hope you're pumped for the version of yourself that's unfolding. Trust the path, the best is yet to come. This is so daggy, but: Cowabunga!

A Letter to 'Future You'

Pen to paper flows free,
Future you, what will you be?

I absolutely love writing letters from the person I am today to the version of myself I'm becoming. Over the years, I've written many letters like this, and now I want to invite you into this space. This is a letter of celebration – of the future wins, the dreams you've brought to life, and the heartfelt goals you've achieved. It's a chance to feel the essence of those dreams coming true, in real time, right now. Manifesting is all about imagining yourself in that space, feeling it as if it's already happened.

Alright, I'll kick things off with a short and sweet letter, writing to myself like it's all already been achieved, then it's going to be your turn!

Dear Lu,

I see you, and I'm incredibly proud of everything you've accomplished. You and your life-long partner are just made for each other – so much fun and so perfectly in sync! You two are a powerhouse team, and it's an absolute heart explosion to see you both together and so funny. What a joy! I adore his kids, too, and can't believe you skipped straight to the best part: being a granny! It's also so awesome that your families get along so well!

Thinking of the incredible life you've built and the body of work you've created fills me with so much admiration. You've worked hard, yes, but it's so clear you've relished every minute of it. What a fun ride it's been, Lu!

Your exquisite home is pure paradise. I can't imagine a more nurturing, magical space. You're absolutely rocking it, divine lady. Now, just kick back, enjoy your amazing books, and keep loving every single moment of this wonderful life you've created with your loves.

All my love,
X Lu

PS: Keep dancing and singing heaps. That dance track album you made is insanely awesome, by the way!

• • •

Writing that letter to myself felt so good and I've gotta say, there are times I've written letters to myself that I am precisely living now. Thank you 'future self' letter-writing activity; thank you, Universe!

Okay, it's your turn now. Go ahead and fill the space with your own dreams and victories. Feel free to blow your own future trumpet really loudly, like I just did! Because, dammit, this is your journal and precious future we're talking about. Dream big!

Dear............

Love from me

SHINE YOUR LIGHT

Vision Board

Get creative here: let yourself shine,
It's all about you, a journey divine!
Build a vision board with desires and dreams,
Add pictures, words, and radiant beams.

Yeehaa! It's vision board time!

Are you as excited as I am? I get such a buzz every time I start preparing for my next vision board. For those who watched *Married at First Sight*, you might remember my scroll: a living, evolving list that I'm constantly updating and using to call in what I desire. Everything on the last vision board I made has all come true, bar one. What?! At the time of writing this journal, I'm still holding out for my everlasting love!

If you've never done one before, think of a vision board as a beautiful collage of the fabulous future you that you're stepping into. Get creative and fill your vision board with images, words, and declarations.

Before you begin, ask yourself, 'What do I truly want?' Explore the endless possibilities before you and reimagine your life. Allow your emotions to guide you in crafting the reality you wish to manifest. Be bold, let the brakes off, and let your imagination lead you!

Feel the energy of your vision. What frequency are you putting out there into the Universe and what are you painting on your canvas?

Ready for bossy me now? I strongly suggest (with love, of course) that you set aside a couple of uninterrupted hours to make your most life-affirming vision board yet! Putting time aside to create a vision board is a ginormous act of self-love that can have a big impact. It's so powerful to articulate and regularly revisit your personal man-i-festo.

There's something immensely energising about gathering bits of inspiration and crafting a visual dreamscape of the life you want to create. Whether you have a paintbrush, colour printer, or a stack of old cards, magazines, and collected treasures, keep this personal and fun and authentically you. Ya ready?! Here's how to get started.

- Gather your tools: scissors, glue, magazines, markers, and a big piece of paper or poster board.

- Set the space and mood: set the vibe with music or a candle and let yourself dream without limits.

- Create your vision: pick words, images, and ideas that spark joy, truth, and excitement.

- Once you're done, display your masterpiece somewhere you'll see it every day. Let it remind you of where you're heading and help you to stay focused on the life you're creating.

- And here's the most important part: the magic happens when you take action to achieve the things you've glued to the page. Start with small, inspired steps daily toward your dreams: that's where it's at. Be pragmatic. Then watch how things begin to shift. The universe will meet you halfway!

So, grab your scissors: snippidy-snip, let's go! xxx

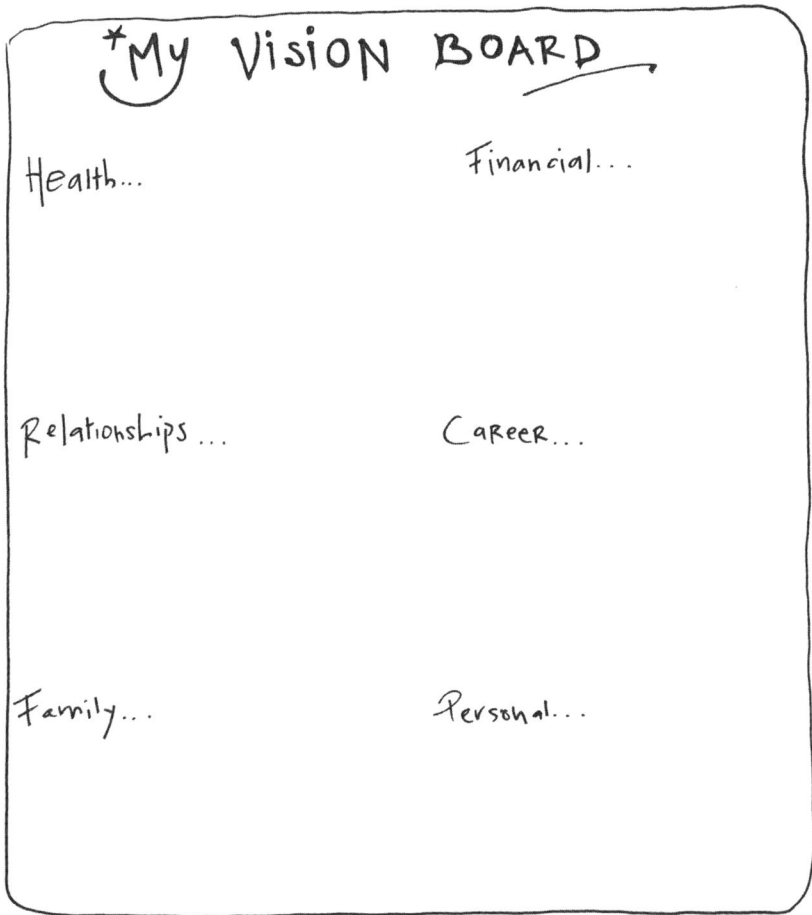

*MY VISION BOARD

Health...   Financial...

Relationships...   Career...

Family...   Personal...

• • •

Once you've created your vision board, I'd love to see what you're calling in for the year ahead. Let's inspire each other – I'll share mine if you share yours! You can post your vision board on the Lucinda Light Community (Official) Facebook page, where fellow deep-divers can comment, encourage, and offer support – all in a space of love and non-judgement. Find us here: www.facebook.com/groups/lucindalightcommunity/ If you're more of an Insta person, tag me on Instagram at @lucindaslight – just know, I might re-share your vision to spread the inspiration even further! Set your vision loose! Now go crush it, you spunk!

Soulful Scribbles & Dribbles!

Feedback-seeking

One who knows others may be wise and astute,
But the ones who know themselves are truly acute.

Alright, ready to push past your comfort zone and plunge into the world of self-awareness through honest feedback? This one's going to require a big dollop of courage! We're talking about reaching out to your people to get some feedback on your emotional intelligence and interpersonal skills (and if they're up for it, make it a two-way exchange!). Self-assessment can be a bit tricky – so why not make it a fun, collaborative process? If things go well, you might want to check in with them again on other areas of growth mentioned in this book. As you evolve, ask them to share any shifts they've noticed in your interactions and how things have changed.

To kick things off, I've put together a list of thoughtful, easy-going questions you can ask your family, friends, or work colleagues. Their insightful responses can really shine a light on areas where you can keep growing and support your journey toward emotional intelligence. Let's make this a fun, honest, positive exchange that helps you step into your best self! Create a sacred space, and ask them:

♥ *How do you perceive my emotional responses in challenging situations?*
Are there areas where you think I could handle emotions more effectively?

♥ *Can you recall a time when I misunderstood your feelings or needs?*
How might I improve my ability to empathise with you in the future?

♥   *What ways do you think I contribute to our relationship positively or negatively?*

♥   *How do you feel I manage stress and pressure? Are there ways you think I could better cope or maintain balance?*

♥   *Is there anything you wish I understood better about your emotions or experiences? How could I be more supportive or attentive to your needs?*

♥   *Can you point out any recurring patterns in my behaviour that might hinder my personal growth or relationships? How could I address these?*

• • •

And there you have it! The power of listening to feedback from those who care about you is undeniable, especially when it's given with love and a genuine desire to support your growth. Embrace accountability, practise self-reflection, and remember to be compassionate with yourself throughout the process or with theirs. These are the keys to evolving into the best version of you. Bring it on!

For the Super-seeker

To the ones who love to go deeper and explore wider: Your curiosity and courage to truly know yourself and others Is what makes life richer and connections more real. Keep being you, Boo!

If you've made it this far, it's clear you're someone who values growth, self-awareness, and deeper soul exploration – and that's exciting! The potential for expansion is limitless.

Over the years, my journey toward self-development and inner peace has been profoundly shaped by the following transformative concepts and life-changing books. These have not only enriched my life but also uncovered aspects of myself I never knew were there. Open your favourite search engine, and see where these take you.

Buyer beware: Ts and Cs apply! You might scratch your head at times and think, *What on Earth does all this mean, Lu?* Or maybe you're buzzing? All these new paths to go down! As a super-seeker, there may be some 'been there, done that', too. Not everything will resonate, but wherever you're at, know this: right now, you're exactly where you're meant to be. Trust your intuition and let the clues that ignite you guide you.

Each suggestion here isn't just a tool – it's an invitation to delve more and to unlock new codes within yourself. These references and systems are entire worlds waiting for you to peruse. They'll take you into the essence of our shared humanity and the unique constellation that makes you *you*.

Ikigai: A Japanese concept to help you find your 'reason for being' by combining what you love, what you're good at, what the world needs, and what you can be paid for.

Your ikigai?

Human Design: Discover your energetic blueprint and learn whether you're a generator, manifestor, projector, reflector, or manifesting generator. It offers insights into how you make decisions, use your energy, and align with your purpose.

What are ya?

Gene Keys: Immerse yourself in this system of personal development that blends astrology, I Ching, and modern genetics. It helps you uncover your unique gifts, shadow aspects, and highest potential to live a fulfilling life.

Soulful scribble reflections:

Enneagram: Explore the nine personality types, such as The Helper, The Achiever, or The Peacemaker, to gain a deeper understanding of your motivations, fears, and core desires.

Drum roll ... and you are ...?

Your numerology: Decode the numbers tied to your birth date and name to uncover your life path, destiny, and personality numbers – insights into your life's purpose and natural traits.

1, 2, 3, go!

Life Path Number (in numerology): Dive into the broader purpose and lessons of your life.

Does it resonate?

Myers–Briggs Type Indicator: Learn your four-letter MBTI type (e.g. INFJ or ESTP) to better understand your preferences for energy (introversion or extraversion), information, decisions, and the world around you.

ABCD INFJ ...?

Soul archetypes: Explore archetypes like The Lover, The Creator, The Warrior, or The Sage to uncover patterns in how you show up in the world.

Archetypes most true to you?

Attachment style: Learn about how you connect and relate in relationships: secure, anxious, avoidant, or a mix.

What's your attachment style?

Ayurvedic dosha type: Explore whether you're predominantly Vata, Pitta, or Kapha, and how this affects your energy and balance.

Radiant reflections:

The Big Five personality traits: A psychology-based breakdown of openness, conscientiousness, extraversion, agreeableness, and neuroticism.

Heartful hindsight:

Your prominent love language: Identify how you give and receive love – through words of affirmation, acts of service, receiving gifts, quality time, or physical touch – and build stronger relationships by understanding yours and those of others.

We should be fluent in all of these languages. Thoughts?

Wealth dynamics profiles: Are you a Star, Creator, Mechanic, Supporter, Deal Maker, Trader, Accumulator, or Lord? Each profile has a unique way of generating wealth and contributing to teams.

What's your main contribution?

Love archetypes: Based on your patterns in romantic relationships, like The Giver, The Seeker, or The Protector.

Go on, love bird!

Astrological moon and rising signs: Go beyond your sun sign for a deeper understanding of your emotions (moon) and how others perceive you (rising). Get your whole natal chart read.

The poetry of astronomy, my favourite. I'm a Cancer sun, Leo moon, Libra ascendant. What's your constellation?

Chinese zodiac sign: Explore the characteristics and elements of your year of birth.

I'm a metal Monkey. What animal are you?

Sensory: Are you more visual, auditory, kinesthetic, or a mix in how you process the world?

I'm mostly kinesthetic. What's your prominent sensory style?

Elemental affinity: Discover your connection to earth, air, fire, water, or spirit and how it reflects your essence.

Drowning, dripping, and diving in with splashes over here. You?

The Window of Tolerance: This is a helpful concept for managing your emotional and physiological responses to stress. It represents your comfort zone for handling emotions effectively.

What did you learn?

Internal Locus of Control: The belief that you are the captain of your ship, steering your life with intention and responsibility. This mindset shifts your focus from external circumstances to your own actions, decisions, and mindset.

Can you captain your own ship?

Meta-Moment: A powerful pause button for your emotions, giving you the space to respond instead of react. It's about stepping back, observing your feelings, and choosing how you want to show up in any given moment.

Reckon you'll practise that?

Nonviolent Communication (NVC): A compassionate approach to communication that fosters understanding, connection, and harmony. Developed by Marshall Rosenberg, NVC helps us express ourselves honestly while empathising with others' feelings and needs.

Is this something you'll look into further?

Drama Triangle: A fascinating model created by Stephen Karpman that reveals the toxic roles we often play in conflicts: Victim, Persecutor, and Rescuer. Understanding this triangle helps us step out of drama and into empowerment.

It's such a good one to be aware of, don't you think?

Empowerment Triangle: The antidote to Karpman's Drama Triangle, created by David Emerald, this framework shifts us from toxic conflict roles to empowered, constructive dynamics. Instead of playing Victim, Persecutor, or Rescuer, the Empowerment Triangle reframes these into Creator, Challenger, and Coach: roles that foster growth and solutions.

Thoughts?

The Four-Step Apology: A heart-centred framework for making amends with authenticity and care. More than just a 'sorry', it's a process to repair trust, take responsibility, and genuinely connect with the person you've hurt. This method ensures your apology lands meaningfully and fosters healing for both parties.

How good is that?

Communication styles: Understanding how you and others communicate is a game-changer. Whether you're an assertive advocate, a passive listener, or somewhere in between, knowing your style – and others' – helps you connect more clearly, resolve conflicts more effectively, and express your needs with greater ease.

What's your predominant?

A huge thanks to the sages who left us a record of the wisdom of the ages. And hooray that said wisdom is still being interpreted, reinvented, and made available to us in endless ways. Being able to access it in our own time and at our own pace is downright magical.

Now, because sharing is caring (and because these gems have seriously rocked my world), here's a list of books that have been absolute paradigm-shifters for me. They've sparked inspiration, opened my perspective, and some of their ideas have even snuck their way into shaping *Shine Your Light*.

The Power of Now – Eckhart Tolle

A New Earth – Eckhart Tolle

The Untethered Soul – Michael A. Singer

The Surrender Experiment – Michael A. Singer

Conversations with God (series) – Neale Donald Walsch

The Boy, the Mole, the Fox and the Horse – Charlie Mackesy

The Artist's Way – Julia Cameron

The Alchemist – Paulo Coelho

Man's Search for Meaning – Viktor E. Frankl

The Hero's Journey – Joseph Campbell

Becoming Supernatural – Dr Joe Dispenza

The Celestine Prophecy – James Redfield

The Seven Spiritual Laws of Success – Deepak Chopra

The Subtle Art of Not Giving a F*ck – Mark Manson

The Road Less Travelled – M. Scott Peck

The Life-changing Magic of Tidying – Marie Kondo

The Five Love Languages – Gary Chapman

The Four Agreements Companion Book – Don Miguel Ruiz

The Fifth Agreement – Don Miguel Ruiz, Don Jose Ruiz, with Janet Mills

Ask and It Is Given – Esther and Jerry Hicks

When Things Fall Apart – Pema Chödrön

How to Win Friends and Influence People – Dale Carnegie

Emotional Intelligence – Daniel Goleman

• • •

Whoa! How many rabbit holes did you tumble down, I wonder?

In my toughest moments – when life felt unbearable and even my body seemed to betray me – books and transformative insights became my lifeline. They showed up like beacons, delivering the wisdom I needed at exactly the right time, lighting up the way and shifting my perspective when I needed it most.

I've learnt to trust that the messages we're meant to hear always find us when our hearts are ready to receive them. My greatest hope is that *Shine Your Light* becomes that for you: a source of comfort, clarity, and a resounding 'YES!' to guide and uplift you on this beautiful journey we're walking together.

Final Words

To the divine you,

I hope this journal has sparked the fire that's already burning within you. The world needs your unique light, and I trust this guide has helped you connect more deeply with the beautiful sparkle-arkle you are. You're incredible for showing up and doing the work. I'm so proud of your courage and commitment!

We're all learning, growing, and supporting one another on this journey back to our truest selves. The beauty of us all blooming together gives me such hope for our collective evolution. This journal is here for you, always. When you feel stagnant, come back. When doubt creeps in, come back...

Keep shedding what no longer serves you. Be gentle, be kind, forgive yourself, and know you're doing your best. Life will throw challenges — and you will experience many a pang, sure — but now you are more resourced and ready for those. Keep finding your tools and exploring your truth.

You carry the love and wisdom of your ancestors, breaking patterns they couldn't, rewriting the story for yourself. You have everything you need to create, celebrate, and reshape your life in ways that nourish your soul and, in turn, others'. I'm endlessly grateful for you, for me, for us – what a gift it is to be alive on this planetary ride.

Thank you for walking this path with me. In a world that often wants to dim our light, to know yourself and boldly shine is an act of rebellion. Let's keep breaking through, together. And if you stumble, reach out, speak up, journal it, mess it up, and create something even more beautiful from the chaos.

This is the human experience – bless this glorious mess. Thank you for being part of it with me. The best is still to come for you – believe it in every cell of your body!

With infinite love and light,
Mumma Lu

PS...

How dare you be so gorgeous!

Acknowledgements

To my incredible circle of readers and supporters: each of you is an irreplaceable thread in this story. You are the soul-seekers, the ones who mirror the love and hope we all carry within us, propelling it forward. Your encouragement, belief, and trust in my words have made this all possible. Knowing that my words have found a home in your hearts is an honour I can't fully express. Thank you for cheering me on with your love, your energy, and your unwavering support – pom poms and all!

To my greatest teachers – my family, both by blood and by choice – thank you for showing me what love, strength, and authenticity truly mean. I am shaped by each of you in ways words can't fully capture. Mum and Dad, Troy, Eliza, and Willow: I love you to bits. You are my heart and soul. To my mum, especially: thank you for being my rock and my greatest inspiration. I am forever grateful for your endless love and support. I wouldn't be here without you.

To HarperCollins, especially Imogen, who took the punt on me: thank you for the honour of bringing my first book to life. Your belief in me is a gift I'll carry always.

To Nathan Stone, my brilliant agent and dear friend at Gallos: thank you for your unwavering belief in me from day one and for navigating the logistics with grace. You've made this journey so much smoother than I could've imagined.

To Anne Reilly, my editor – thank you for pushing me to dig deeper into my writing, for your experience, and for believing in me even when things got chaotic.

A huge thank you to Channel 9 and Endemol Shine for welcoming me as a Season 11 *Married at First Sight Australia* bride. It has been an incredible platform to share my love, light, and offerings with a bigger audience. I'm forever grateful for this life-changing opportunity.

And to all the teachers, sages, and writers whose words have lit my path over the years – thank you for sharing your wisdom and elevating us all. Your words continue to remind us of our power and potential.

About the Author

Holistic counsellor, marriage celebrant, speaker, and MC, Lucinda Light wowed the world with her voice of reason, compassion, and mediation skills while starring on *Married at First Sight Australia,* Season 11. Lucinda brought her tour, 'An Evening with Lucinda Light', to sold-out UK, Irish, and Australian theatres, and appeared in Channel 4's *The Honesty Box* as the Sincerity Coach – mentoring Truetopians and facilitating holistic activities to foster authentic personal growth. Now, she continues sharing her emotional intelligence with her debut book, *Shine Your Light*